Praise for *An Unexplainable Life*

An Unexplainable Life is more than a Bible study; it is a transformational fifty-day experience with God that will open your mind to a fresh understanding of Scripture and the power of the Holy Spirit. Erica Wiggenhorn will inspire you, equip you, and challenge you to not only learn the Word but live it *boldly.* A must have resource for every church and women's ministry desiring to be courageous followers of Christ who turn the world upside down like the early church.

KATHE WUNNENBERG
Author, speaker, mentor, and founder of Hopelifters Unlimited

I have been a pastor for over eighteen years and reading *An Unexplainable Life* was like a breath of fresh air for my heart. Erica captures the deep longing we have when we love the church and yet long for something more, something deeper, something authentic and real. It's not something new we long for, but rather a restoration of the joy and awe of life in Christ. Biblically robust and warmly personal, *An Unexplainable Life* will be like sitting down with a friend to consider the deep things of God together.

MATT VALENCIA
Lead Pastor, ReGeneration Church, Scotts Valley, CA

If you're longing for more out of your Christian life, dive into the book of Acts with Erica Wiggenhorn. Dare to ask the Holy Spirit to open your mind and awaken your heart to all that He has for you to embrace. Erica brings Scripture alive with purpose and passion!

BECKY HARLING
International speaker and the author of *The 30-Day Praise Challenge*

Erica Wiggenhorn's heart for connecting women to a deeper and greater understanding of biblical truth beats across the pages in her new Bible study, *An Unexplainable Life.* Her fresh, biblically sound teaching will help you gain new perspective while transforming and strengthening your faith.

SARA HORN
Speaker and author of *My So-Called Life as a Proverbs 31 Wife*

One hundred and twenty simple, ordinary people were gathered together in a room when the Holy Spirit came and incredibly, wonderfully, and unexplainably empowered them to go change a world! He changed their lives and He changed the city, region, and world through the message they shared and lives they lived. He wants to do it again, today, through you and me. He wants us to live an unexplainable life of power, mission, and perseverance! You will be blessed by this study from Erica Wiggenhorn and challenged to allow Him to live through you an unexplainable life!

STEPHEN ENGRAM
Senior Pastor, Desert Springs Community Church, Goodyear, AZ
Executive Director of Southwest Church Connection, CBAmerica

Ready to go deeper? Erica Wiggenhorn takes us on a journey to "deeper" in the verse-by-verse trek through Acts 1–12. Anytime we come to God's Word with a yearning to let Him change us by it, we're simply never the same. And Erica approaches this powerful passage with authenticity, clarity, and a sweet savvy, heading us straight for that change. Biblical, historical, easy to engage—the whole package. We're not talking about a little dusting across the surface here. Erica shows us those deep places and offers us practical helps in how to walk out our faith. Gear up for some spiritual spelunking!

RHONDA RHEA
TV host and author of ten books including *Espresso Your Faith*

Erica Wiggenhorn whets the appetite of the reader to move from a vanilla Christian experience to an unexplainable adventure that is based in biblical truth and authored by the Holy Spirit. This well-written, integrative study challenges every Christ follower with something more—an unexplainable adventure based on God's Word and authored by God's Spirit. A must-read for every person who longs to be used of God to make an eternal difference.

DOUG SCHMIDT
Pastor of Woodside Bible Church, Troy, MI

an Unexplainable Life:

RECOVERING THE WONDER AND DEVOTION
OF THE EARLY CHURCH (ACTS 1–12)

ERICA WIGGENHORN

MOODY PUBLISHERS

CHICAGO

Unless otherwise indicated, Scripture quotations are from the ESV® Bible (The Holy Bible, English Standard Version®), copyright © 2001 by Crossway, a publishing ministry of Good News Publishers. Used by permission. All rights reserved.

Scripture quotations marked HCSB are taken from the Holman Christian Standard Bible®, Copyright © 1999, 2000, 2002, 2003, 2009 by Holman Bible Publishers. Used by permission. HCSB® is a federally registered trademark of Holman Bible Publishers.

Scripture quotations marked NASB are taken from the New American Standard Bible®, Copyright © 1960, 1962, 1963, 1968, 1971, 1972, 1973, 1975, 1977, 1995 by The Lockman Foundation. Used by permission. (www. Lockman.org) Scripture quotations marked NIV are taken from the Holy Bible, New International Version®, NIV®. Copyright © 1973, 1978, 1984, 2011 by Biblica, Inc.™ Used by permission of Zondervan. All rights reserved worldwide. www.zondervan.com. The "NIV" and "New International Version" are trademarks registered in the United States Patent and Trademark Office by Biblica, Inc.™

Scripture quotations marked NLT are taken from the Holy Bible, New Living Translation, copyright © 1996, 2004, 2007, 2013 by Tyndale House Foundation. Used by permission of Tyndale House Publishers, Inc., Carol Stream, Illinois 60188. All rights reserved.

Edited by Pam Pugh
Interior design: Erik M. Peterson
Cover design: Dean Renninger
Cover image of watercolor copyright © by LoveKay/Adobe Stock (63424683). All rights reserved.
Author photo: Suzanne Busta

Library of Congress Cataloging-in-Publication Data

Names: Wiggenhorn, Erica, author.
Title: An unexplainable life : recovering the wonder and devotion of the
   early church (Acts 1-12) / Erica Wiggenhorn.
Description: Chicago : Moody Publishers, 2016.
Identifiers: LCCN 2016004439 | ISBN 9780802414731
Subjects: LCSH: Bible. Acts, I-XI--Textbooks. | Church renewal.
Classification: LCC BS2626 .W54 2016 | DDC 226.6/06--dc23 LC record available at https://lccn.loc.gov/2016004439

We hope you enjoy this book from Moody Publishers. Our goal is to provide high-quality, thought-provoking books and products that connect truth to your real needs and challenges. For more information on other books and products written and produced from a biblical perspective, go to www.moodypublishers.com or write to:

Moody Publishers
820 N. LaSalle Boulevard
Chicago, IL 60610

1 3 5 7 9 10 8 6 4 2

Printed in the United States of America

This book is affectionately dedicated to

The Bravo Team—my first and forever true church.

All of the pastors and saints at Desert Springs Community Church.

Your teaching, fellowship, love, and encouragement
have continually spurred me on.

May the unexplainable happen within and among us!

CONTENTS

LET'S OPEN OUR MINDS

"Then he opened their minds to understand the Scriptures."
—Luke 24:45

Welcome to *An Unexplainable Life: Recovering the Wonder and Devotion of the Early Church.*

Acts is the place where all the teachings of Jesus come to life in living color before our eyes. After three years of traveling with Jesus, walking in His footsteps, yet struggling to fully grasp the magnitude of His mission, the apostles' awakening arrives. They still held misconceptions and were bound in understanding by the culture and events surrounding them, but they slowly started to become privy to their own limited perceptions. Their minds were awakened to the fact that they still had much to learn from their beloved Jesus. They hadn't yet figured it all out.

The Holy Spirit comes and the disciples are utterly transformed. Men of doubt, full of disbelief and fear, become courageous giants filled with wisdom and truth. Their own ambitions are abandoned, risking everything for the message and mission of Christ. Circumstances matter not. Christ has become their only reality.

And their deepest desire was Christ becoming *everyone's* only reality.

Maybe it's time that you and I boldly pray for Christ to open our minds and give us a fresh understanding of the Scriptures. Maybe it's time for you and me to admit that we haven't yet figured it all out. Cultural influences, circumstances, and our own misconceptions have stifled the life of God in us, resulting in imprecise views of Christ's mission for our lives both individually and in the Christian church collectively. We have become men and women of doubt and fear. We search for courageous giants of the faith, but we cannot find them. Our prayers have become focused solely on our own individual needs. We are consumed by our circumstances.

What if Christ were to become my greatest reality?

What if His message and mission were my deepest desire?

Would my worry, anxiety, unrest, discontent, and angst be replaced by the abiding reality of the Prince of Peace ruling in my heart and mind?

Do I truly believe that losing my life for His sake results in the greatest discovery of all time?

If you answered no to the last question, this study will challenge you. If you answered yes, I pray this study will equip you and bring an awakening of the reality of Christ into view, dimming everyone and everything else within your sight. I pray that the words of Jesus will come alive to you in new ways you've never understood before. And that when your mind becomes open, you will go and tell. You will become witnesses to what you have heard. Not timid "suggesters" of the truth, but courageous giants—full of wisdom and truth, prepared to turn the world upside down.

". . . grant to your servants to continue to speak your word with all boldness" (Acts 4:29).

Let's be brave together.

MAKING THE MOST OF THIS STUDY

Over the next fifty days, we are going to become eyewitnesses of the birth of the early church. As we walk alongside Peter in the first twelve chapters of Acts, we will discover a radically transformed man. My prayer is that you and I are transformed as well. In only fifty days Peter went from a timid man, full of fear and hiding in the shadows, to a courageous follower of Jesus. The change was unexplainable, a work of God in Peter's heart and mind, because as those around him noted: Peter had been with Jesus.

What do you suppose God could do in and through each of us in fifty days if we spent time with Jesus in this study of His Word? I encourage you to find out!

Will you join me in the journey of completing five days of homework each week? To maximize the learning time and allow you to listen to God, *begin your study time with prayer*, inviting the Holy Spirit to speak to you. Also, try to study on a daily basis. This allows ample time to contemplate the content and develop a habit of getting alone with God regularly, strengthening your relationship with Him.

Beginning on Day 2, each day's session starts with a thematic title and Bible passage that will take you about twenty to thirty minutes to complete. Begin your study time by reading the passage in its entirety. *Read the daily passage aloud*. I've used the English Standard Version as my main text and indicate other versions where applicable, but you may of course use any version you're comfortable with. Reading the daily verses will offer a basic overview of that day's Scripture and story before we break it down more in-depth. The more you familiarize yourself with the verses, the more likely you will remember them and allow their truths to penetrate your heart.

Making your way through each daily assignment, you will encounter several questions in blue. These questions can help you stop, pray, collect your thoughts, and write out answers. Writing responses prompts you to slow down and grapple with the Scriptures, and apply them to your life. On certain days, you will notice blue picture frames. These are your invitation to press pause and dwell in the truths presented that day. Draw, write, doodle, or ponder, allowing the Holy Spirit to speak to you in the quietness of your heart. Bible study is not meant to be a task to complete. Instead, it is an avenue for building a relationship with God. Invest time toward your relationship with Him.

Some of the blue questions can also be used in small group discussions. The leader's guide for this study indicates which questions work best for groups. You can access this free resource at www.ericawiggenhorn.com.

A bonus for you, Deeper Discoveries, has some extra material that corresponds with each week's study. This is an optional component in which you can dig more deeply into the Scriptures by making connections between the Old and New Testaments. You'll find this at www.ericawiggenhorn.com.

I am praying for you as you walk this journey. I pray that God will speak to you, encourage your heart, and build up your faith! I would love to hear what you learn, so please visit me at www.ericawiggenhorn.com and tell me about your progress and insights.

Erica

living an unexplainable life

WEEK 1 | DAY 1
MISSION IMPOSSIBLE

When our Lord looked at us, He saw not only what we were—He was faithful in seeing what we could become! He took away the curse of being and gave us the glorious blessing of becoming.

—*A. W. Tozer*[1]

In only fifty days Peter becomes radically transformed. From being a man crouching in the shadows who denies even knowing Jesus, to becoming a bold preacher proclaiming the resurrection of Jesus in the middle of the temple courts, Peter is a new man. How did the change occur? And more importantly, can such a change occur within us—today, in the here and now?

For the next fifty days, you and I are going to dwell in the first twelve chapters of Acts. In this portion of Scripture we meet Peter face to face and encounter the source of his power. We become challenged to grab hold of that power ourselves, believing that God wants to do something in and through us that is unexplainable apart from Him. Let's give God fifty days and see what He might do! How about it, friend—are you game?

The purpose of this study is not simply to reiterate a message. You can find many Bible studies on the book of Acts. Our purpose here is to reignite a *movement* of the power of the Holy Spirit in each of us individually and in our churches collectively. As Obadiah said to Elijah, "The Spirit of the Lord will carry you I know not where" (1 Kings 18:12). Indeed! No one knows but the Spirit Himself. But unlike the case in Elijah's day, the Spirit has already come. If you have put your faith in the death and resurrection of Jesus Christ, the Spirit now dwells inside you (1 Corinthians 12:7). So where does He want to take you? Where does He want to take your church? The Holy Spirit desires to be a manifest presence in your life to authenticate Christ's claims as Lord.

Here's the thing. The disciples understood from the beginning that Christ had called them to be a part of a movement. Each one of them jumped at the opportunity. What they didn't understand was the *mission* of the movement. They thought they were pursuing civic and social change, not individual change that would result in a universal overhaul of the entire world.

As Christians we, too, fundamentally understand that Jesus has called us to be a part of His movement. We have tapped into Christ's mission for individual change in each of our lives—and we like that part. The problem is that many of us haven't embraced His bold claims that our individual change will result in turning the world upside down. Maybe once the kingdom reached us individually, we became satisfied. As long as Jesus added something to each of our lives personally, we felt good. Therefore, if we become better people as we try to live by scriptural principles, we believe we have fulfilled our mission.

Can I rock your world for a moment? If that is how you and I approach our mission as disciples of Jesus Christ, then *we've missed the mission.* We've made it too small and self-focused. We've sought our own betterment and advancement through His kingdom, but then reflect, "I thought I signed up to be part of something that was bigger than myself," and wonder if something went wrong.

Well, thankfully you did!

But sometimes many of us lose our way and make it all about ourselves. As a result, we forfeit our power. See, the Holy Spirit was sent to authenticate Christ's claims of deity (John 16:14–15). The Spirit powerfully manifests Himself in order for Christ's prayers that the church will demonstrate an unexplainable love for Him and for one another are fulfilled (John 17:20–26). Yet we can lose our dependence on the Holy Spirit and attempt to manufacture our own power.

Here's the remedy: "Then he opened their minds to understand the Scriptures" (Luke 24:45). The Holy Spirit's desire is to continue to magnify Christ. He is our Counselor who guides us into all truth. He is the One who enables us to understand the Scriptures. He is the One who empowers us to live out the mission. *You will be My witnesses. Your life was meant to authenticate My power!* He is able to work in and through us so the world may know the power of Christ.

Are we brave enough to admit that there may be some things we have misunderstood?

Over and over again in the story of Acts, we read of people being in awe of the believers' lives, astonished at their courage, baffled by their wisdom, and in admiration of their lifestyle. Francis Chan writes: "I don't want my life to be explainable without the Holy Spirit. I want people to look at my life and know that I couldn't be doing this by my own power. I want to live in such a way that I am desperate for Him to come through."[2]

Oh, that this would be my heart's cry!

How about you? Are you up for an unexplainable life? Being a witness for Christ means we verify His claims. We demonstrate His power. We embrace that Christ's mission is so much bigger than ourselves and finally fess up that we are "sick to death of ourselves already." We begin to live in such a way that the world's people are left scratching their heads. We leave them baffled.

Acts is the story of Christ's mission becoming reality in the lives of His followers. To study it is an invitation for it to become your reality and mine. Let's get started, shall we?

You may be a brand-new Christian, so this next exercise may be a little difficult for you to complete. I hope it excites you, though, and stirs within you an anticipation of what Christ wants to do in and through your life.

If you're not yet a believer, I hope these questions whet your appetite to know Him!

Let's take a trip down memory lane. Let's breathe in the sweet fragrance of Christ's presence in your life. Recapture some of the moments when Jesus was very much a reality in your daily life.

List three or four specific answers to prayer you have experienced. Perhaps some of the answers were no, and you now understand why.

List a few times when God obviously directed your path through detours, closed doors, or opened doors.

List some times when you unexplainably felt God's presence or power.

List three or four passages of Scripture that jumped off the page and spoke to you in your time of need.

List a few people God graciously brought into your life to teach you truth. (These could be a pastor/author/teacher/speaker, as well as a direct relationship.)

Dear one, these are *some* of the ways the Holy Spirit demonstrates His power and presence in our lives. Please do not be discouraged if you cannot answer them all. Obadiah was right: We do not know where the Spirit will take us. But we know He is here—living inside us. Let's invite Him to speak, guide, direct, and teach us new discoveries about the One He loves to exalt: *Jesus.* Let's embrace an unexplainable life.

JUST WHAT THE DOCTOR ORDERED

Please read aloud ACTS 1:1

Here we are on Day 2 and we haven't even opened up the book of Acts yet! So let's jump right in.

Look at Acts 1:1.

How many books has the author of Acts written?

To whom is he addressing this current work?

What was the subject matter of his first book?

Scripture gives us strong clues as to who wrote the book of Acts in this opening verse. Read Luke 1:1–4 and record the commonalities you see between Luke's opening paragraph in his gospel and Acts 1:1.

Luke was a Gentile. In fact, he is the only Gentile author in the New Testament and by trade he was a physician (Colossians 4:14). I find this interesting because I am married to a doctor. Luke's scientific background provides great insight into his approach in writing not only the gospel of Luke, but also the book of Acts. He writes in the same systematic manner as my husband, Jonathan, does.

When Jonathan first sees a patient, he does several things to arrive at a diagnosis. First, he takes an overall look at the patient. Does he appear generally healthy with only the specific ailment in question plaguing him, or does his health seem compromised in multiple areas? From there, Jonathan takes an assessment of a variety of possible symptoms by posing a litany of questions to the patient, taking all the answers and putting them together as one would arrange puzzle pieces to form a final picture. Once he is certain he has gathered all of the pertinent facts, the doctor finally arrives at a diagnosis. He then develops a treatment plan to restore the patient to health.

This is the approach Luke takes in his writing. By diligently researching all the facts regarding Jesus, he arrives at his verdict: "You may have certainty concerning the things you have been taught" (Luke 1:4). Jesus is indeed the Christ. By the end of the book of Luke, he is firm in this conclusion. From there, he moves on to Acts: the treatment plan. Acts lays out for Theophilus the steps that the followers of Jesus took based on their conclusion that Jesus was indeed the promised Messiah. It is the treatment plan for a disciple.

In a physician's mind, a diagnosis is meaningless if the patient remains untreated. It is the treatment plan that makes the knowledge of the diagnosis worthwhile. Thus it is for Luke: "I have dealt with all that Jesus **began** to do and to teach" (Acts 1:1, emphasis mine). Keep reading, Theophilus. We're talking about more than just an intellectual understanding that Jesus is the Messiah. Did you get that, friend? Accepting Jesus as your Savior is just the beginning.

Luke continued this intense investigation as he wrote Acts. He interviewed the original disciples and other witnesses firsthand. For example, the book of Luke tells a lot about Mary, the mother of Jesus. Perhaps he sat down across from her and asked her to tell her story.

We will see that Luke went to great personal lengths to gather all of the facts firsthand, often putting his own life at risk. For the majority of the book of Acts, Luke writes in the first person, letting us know that he is recording the events as an eyewitness in real time. When he was not present, he switches to the third person, making it clear which events he experienced firsthand.

This determination to conduct such exhaustive research leaves us wondering who Theophilus may have been.

How does Luke address him in Luke 1:3?

How is he addressed in Acts 1:1?

There are competing ideas about Theophilus. His name in Greek means "loved by God" or "friend of God," so some have sought to depersonalize him and conclude that Luke's audience is anyone and everyone who loves God. However, I don't believe this is so. First of all, to address someone as "most excellent" refers to someone of high authority in the Roman world. Luke uses the term twice later in the book of Acts, in reference to Felix (24:2) and to Festus (26:25).

So why does Luke disregard this address in his second book? Some possible explanations are that Theophilus became a Christian after reading Luke's gospel. Out of reverence for the lordship of Christ, he felt unworthy to continue to tout earthly titles of power and authority. Or due to his political position, maybe he wished to maintain his anonymity. And perhaps by this time Luke's relationship with him had deepened, and a formal title wasn't necessary. Or maybe it's not significant at all. We could speculate for days, but due to Luke's two different manners in how he addresses him, I believe Theophilus was an actual person.

In any case, Theophilus is not the most important figure in our story. If we were to indelibly print *one particular word* in this verse in our minds as we begin this journey in Acts, it is the one following the word "Jesus." Read Acts 1:1 again carefully and fill in the following:

All that (everything) Jesus _____ to do and to teach . . .

Today, my friend, is a new beginning. My prayer is that when you finish this study and set it on your shelf, you will say, "That was the time when Jesus *began* to do and to teach me . . ."

We covered a lot today, but before you put your book away, stop and reflect:

If someone were to examine all of the facts and details of your life, would they diagnose you as a Christian? Why or why not?

How has becoming a Christian changed your treatment plan—the way you live your life?

What is one thing you are hoping Jesus may begin to teach you or do in your life as you make your way through this study?

Thank you for the courage to take this journey toward an unexplainable life with me. I am honored that you are here.

WE'VE ONLY JUST BEGUN

Please read aloud ACTS 1:1–5

Luke made it clear to us yesterday that his gospel set out to prove that Jesus was indeed the Christ. All that Theophilus had been taught about him was true. Acts picks up right where Luke's gospel ends.

I liken the two books to the ways my husband and our children approach their gifts on Christmas morning. When Eliana and Nathan run out to our family room and behold all of those wrapped presents under the tree, they cannot wait to get their hands on them! As soon as the paper is ripped from a package and they discover what is underneath, though, they immediately begin to scan the tree to see if there is another wrapped surprise with their name on it. Herein describes the gospel of Luke. Theophilus has unwrapped the mystery of Christ and now knows who He is, but rather than immediately set Him aside, Luke challenges him to more closely examine *all* that He is.

This is how my husband, Jonathan, approaches a Christmas gift. Once it is opened, he rolls it over in his hands, examining it from every angle. He removes the manual (it's usually some sort of gadget or electronic device) and begins to pore through it, discovering all the capabilities of the object. He wants to know every last detail about what it can do and how to best use it. He wants to understand how it works. This is the book of Acts: Jesus at work in your life.

Read Acts 1:2–3.

Where does Luke's gospel end?

How does Jesus now give instructions to His disciples?

Jesus began His work on earth as recorded in the Gospels. He died and rose again, but He was still teaching and working. Though He had conquered sin and death through His crucifixion and resurrection, He still had more to explain to His disciples, and He was commissioning them to carry on His work.

What did Jesus prove to His disciples?

About what did Jesus instruct His disciples?

It was of utmost importance that there was no doubt in the disciples' minds that Jesus had, in fact, risen from the dead in a bodily resurrection. It was also important for the spread of the gospel. While many would claim that the disciples only imagined that Jesus had actually risen from the dead, the early church writers share several examples verifying that Jesus was actually physically alive for forty days after His resurrection.

According to Luke 24:1–12, to whom did Jesus appear first?

> Jesus remained on the earth forty days after His resurrection. In Jewish thought, the number forty often symbolized the fulfillment of a promise or the accomplishment of God's purposes.

Who else did He appear to that same day? (Luke 24:13–35)

When the disciples were still in hiding, how many times did He appear to them? See John 20:24–30.

See John 21:1. Where else did He appear to His disciples?

Read 1 Corinthians 15:1–8. After He had appeared to His disciples on several occasions, who else saw Him?

What promise was going to be fulfilled soon? (Acts 1:4–5)

In case they weren't sure what He meant, what did He specifically say the gift was?

Read Joel 2:28–29 and explain how the gift of the Holy Spirit was the fulfillment of a promise.

Refer to John 16:5–11. In what way would the gift of the Holy Spirit be a form of judgment?

The day that this marvelous gift of the Holy Spirit arrived was a greatly significant one on the Jewish calendar. It was fifty days after Passover. On this holiday, Pentecost, the Jewish people brought wheat sacrifices to the temple. They celebrated the covenant God made with Israel when He gave the Ten Commandments to Moses on Mt. Sinai. The Holy Spirit's arrival ushered in *aspects* of a new covenant. Additional promises of the new covenant will be fulfilled when Christ returns to earth again.

What did Jesus call the true bread of heaven in John 6:32–33?

Describe the new covenant God will make with His people Israel (see Jeremiah 31:31–34).

God divinely orchestrated the death and resurrection of His Son to occur at a time when Jewish people from around the world would converge on Jerusalem in celebration of these holidays. He had instituted these holidays thousands of years prior, commanding that they be migratory feasts in which all adult Jewish men must return to the Holy City of Jerusalem. The holidays foreshadowed His ultimate plan of redemption in the death and resurrection of His Son.

The coming of the promised Holy Spirit was to be no different. This holiday of Pentecost, when He unleashed His power on the apostles, was also a migratory feast. No one who was committed to God was going to miss the scene. Everything was unfolding exactly as God had planned.

What does God say about Himself in Isaiah 46:9–10?

Friend, know this today: God is not finished yet. He has a purpose for your life. He wants to give you an *unexplainable* life. His timeline is unfolding just as He has planned. Don't give up. Don't get discouraged. Don't run ahead of Him. Just wait. The gifts He has for you will arrive right on time. We've only just begun.

Take time to think about what having an "unexplainable life" might look like for you personally. Record your thoughts below.

WEEK 1 | DAY 4
THE GAME PLAN
Please read aloud ACTS 1:6–9

Have you ever been in the middle of telling someone something when they suddenly interrupt you with what feels like a random question? Not only do you wonder if they heard a word you said, but you also question how valuable they find your information to be! This is exactly what the disciples did to Jesus in our passage of Scripture today. Jesus had important instructions to give them during some of their final moments together. He was trying to explain to them the importance of the Holy Spirit's arrival, but they interrupted Him with questions regarding their own agenda.

See Acts 1:6–7.
What question did the disciples ask Jesus?

How did Jesus respond?

The disciples are still seeking a literal kingdom in which Jesus serves as king and they get handed some official titles of importance. Jesus had told them when He set up His kingdom, His twelve disciples would sit on thrones judging the twelve tribes of Israel. (See Matthew 19:28.) The mother of James and John requested that her sons' thrones be in the most special places of honor (Matthew 20:21). They expected a literal kingdom, its arrival imminent, and one in which they would hold special positions of authority. No wonder Jesus admonished them to not be like the Gentiles in how they govern (Matthew 20:25–28). Here are the real questions they have:

So when is my payout? When do we begin ruling?

Have You figured out what my role is going to be yet, Jesus?

Are You finally going to take some of that miraculous power of Yours and use it to overthrow the Romans?

We've followed You around for three years now. When are You going to get with the game plan, Jesus?

Actually, guys, He's trying to give you the game plan, but you're interrupting Him with your self-absorbed questions! The disciples still did not understand the spiritual nature of Christ's kingdom. Maybe today we have gone too far in the opposite direction. We have focused so much on the spiritual aspect of the kingdom that it is nearly invisible to the world. We have ceased to expect the power of the Holy Spirit to be lived out in a literal and tangible way before our eyes. We have failed to understand that the way we live our lives is supposed to serve as proof of the kingdom.

Christ gives us the power to overcome self—to put an end to our selfish ambitions and desires and to serve one another in love. Jesus is trying to explain to them that through the gift of the Holy Spirit they will accomplish this, but they are still wrapped up in their own agendas.

We ask Jesus these same questions, they just sound a little different. We might say:

I've been obedient. Why aren't You blessing me?

Why are You making my life so hard? My coworker is unreliable, but he gets a raise!

Why won't You allow me to serve in the area I want to in the church? Why does that Jessica always get to be in charge of everything?

When are You going to intervene on my behalf, Jesus? I've waited a long time.

You know I've always had it on my heart to _____, Jesus. Why aren't You making it happen for me? When are You going to get with my game plan?

Jesus jolts them back into attention by making it plain that the timeline of His earthly kingdom is none of their concern. Likewise, the timeline of Jesus meeting our agendas is none of our concern. He is trying to shift our focus to more important things.

What did Jesus say they would receive in Acts 1:8?

What would they become as a result?

Where would they go?

FIRST:

SECOND:

THIRD:

FOURTH:

I've got news for you, friend. This power that Jesus is talking about is the Greek word *dunamis*. It is where we get the word "dynamite." It is the same word used to describe the power that God used in raising Christ from the dead. This isn't a shot in the arm, a little *ummph* kind of power—this is earth-shattering stuff. Am I petty enough to be upset because someone else was chosen to lead worship or teach? I hope not! This is power that can drastically shift our focus from everything that pulls us down and wastes our energy.

Let's take a closer look at what the disciples were to do with that power—become witnesses.

The disciples held the authority to be His witnesses because they themselves had *witnessed* Christ, spending three years following Him everywhere, seeing how He lived, and listening to what He taught. In the time of Jesus, followers of a rabbi did this in order to *become like their teacher,* imitating in every way imaginable his lifestyle and teaching. What they lacked was the power to become like Christ and have their lives reflect all that He had taught them to be and to do. Remember what Jesus told them? "You, therefore, must be perfect" (Matthew 5:48).

Who in the world could live up to that? They also had yet to be able to *avoid something*: namely, their own selfish ambitions and desires. They were not yet ready to abandon everything for a kingdom that offered little tangible reward in the here and now. They still did not understand the emotional and spiritual rewards Jesus offered.

One benefit was that they were going to get to travel! Okay, I'm being facetious here—because when Jesus said they were going to be His witnesses "to the end of the earth," it may have startled them. It's likely none of them had ever left Israel except for the times when Jesus took them to Caesarea Philippi and Sidon. And Samaria? Who wanted to go there? Yet Jesus was saying they were to go to places unimaginable and engage those with whom they had formerly been forbidden to eat or associate. They were to dine with pagans and speak to people of foreign tongue—ministering to people they had been taught to disdain and look down on. They were even supposed to witness to their enemies. Sounds a lot different than their agenda, doesn't it?

No wonder they were going to need some dynamite power! How were they going to humble themselves enough to serve these people? If you are guessing they missed what Jesus said, you're right. They didn't get it. "He couldn't possibly mean it," they thought. "He must mean Jews that live in other parts of the world, not pagan idolaters. Right?" (We will understand this more fully when we arrive in Acts 11.)

Will you be brave enough to ask Jesus what His game plan for your life is?

Did it ever cross your mind that Jesus might want you to cross the socioeconomic tracks and drive across town to another neighborhood that is more ethnically diverse than your own—or perhaps reach out to people with other belief systems? Where are you willing to go to be a witness for Christ?

Spend some time in prayer asking God these two questions and record what He reveals to you below:

WHILE WE WAIT

Please read aloud ACTS 1:9–14

As I read through the book of Acts, I am convinced that it is plausible Luke became a convert to Judaism before he became a Christian. The phraseology he uses and his manner of describing events correlate directly to significant moments in the Old Testament. It is also further proof that the Word of God is inspired because it allows readers over two thousand years later to make the same connections.

Read Acts 1:9 (HCSB) and circle the word(s) that describe Jesus' ascension:

> After He had said this, He was taken up as they were watching, and a cloud took Him out of their sight.

The prophet Elijah had been "taken" to heaven in a chariot of fire (2 Kings 2:11), and the Jews of Jesus' day expected Elijah to accompany the Messiah's return (Malachi 4:5). This reference to Jesus being "taken up" would have clicked in the Jews' minds that Jesus had gone back to heaven just like Elijah had.

The cloud was also significant for other reasons. In the wilderness where the Jews wandered after their escape from Egypt, the Shekinah glory of God rested in the cloud to guide them. Paul equates the Shekinah Spirit of God with the Holy Spirit living inside of us in 1 Corinthians 3:16. First-century Jews equated it with the presence of God. In other words, it was as though God Himself came in the cloud and carried His Son back to heaven where His throne awaited Him! We have to remember that at this point in Israel's history, the Holy Spirit of God had been poured out on one person at a time to fulfill a specific purpose. The disciples did not yet comprehend the universal dispensation of the Holy Spirit that was soon to occur. God's coming in the cloud brought the disciples reassurance that Jesus was completing His mission from God. For thirty-three years the Father had witnessed

His Son experience the plagues of life on earth: temptation, illness, rejection, betrayal, and even death. Imagine His joy when the penalty had fully been paid and His Son was to return to glory!

Another Old Testament passage, foretelling about Christ, mentions clouds.

How is Jesus described in Daniel's vision in Daniel 7:13–14?

These references to Old Testament prophecies were Luke's way of confirming that Jesus was the Messiah, the fulfillment of visions and prophecies of long before. Luke brings his Grecian background into his writing as well. Consider this commonly held belief in Roman paganism:

> Many of Luke's readers would know that when a Roman emperor died, it had been customary to declare that someone had seen his soul escaping from his body and going up to heaven. If you go to the top end of the Forum in Rome, stand under the Arch of Titus, and look up, you will see a carving of the soul of Titus, who was emperor in the 80s in the first century, ascending to heaven. The message of this was clear: the emperor was becoming a god (thus enabling his son and heir to style himself "son of god," which is a useful title if you want to run the world).[3]

Luke's reference to this pagan belief presents Jesus as superior to these Roman gods. They believed that the emperor's *soul* would ascend to heaven; Jesus was physically resurrected and His *body and soul* were being raised up to rule and reign. Greek philosophy viewed the body as inherently evil; Jesus' bodily resurrection speaks of His power over *death and evil*. In other words, Jesus superseded any god-like capabilities that the Roman emperors might claim for themselves. He was the One, the only One, who held the true authority and power. Greek philosophy and religion pervaded the Roman Empire during the first century, necessitating the explanation of Jesus' supremacy over all other Roman and Greek gods. Additionally, many of the Jewish people had been dispersed throughout the Roman Empire at this time, and had become deeply influenced by Greek culture and philosophy.

Scripture often refers to these Jewish people as Hellenistic Jews.

See Acts 1:10–11. Describe what is happening.

Jesus was last glorified on the Mount of Olives. Afterward, He returned with the disciples to continue His ministry (Luke 9:28–37). I'm sure they hoped it was the same in this instance. They still had so much they didn't understand. Why did Jesus have to go away? Christ had already explained to them why He had to depart.

What had He told them in John 16:7?

The two messengers (angels) were clear. Jesus was going to return in the same way He left. It wasn't going to be some secret event they could miss. It was going to be as plain as day. Now they were to go and wait as He had said. I'm sure they were racking their brains trying to remember all that He had told them about the Holy Spirit. I'm sure they argued and debated with one another over what they remembered. But they obeyed. They went back to the room and they waited.

List the names of the eleven disciples who were there:

Who else was with them? (See Acts 1:14.)

What did they do while they waited?

It is interesting to note that Jesus' siblings were now there with the disciples. As far as we know, none of them had been at His crucifixion. Had He appeared to them after His resurrection? We know He appeared to James (1 Corinthians 15:7), but Scripture does not mention others.

I find it so beautiful that they prayed during this time of waiting. It was ten days of continual prayer as this ragtag bunch sought God with everything they had. What was going to happen when the Holy Spirit came? I wonder if they were praying for God to speed the Holy Spirit's coming much like we eagerly pray for Christ's return. Unlike the time when they left their room prior to the ascension and returned to their livelihood of fishing (John 21:1–3), this time the disciples remained together, praying constantly for God to show them what to do next.

And show them He would! But that is for next week. For now, let's stop and do a little reflection.

Are you waiting on something from God—an answer, direction, or clarity? Write about that here or in a journal.

Have you devoted the matter to prayer? Write out your prayer.

Who are some other believers you could invite to pray with you about the matter?

As we learned yesterday, God's timing has a very distinct purpose. His reasons for making us wait are far beyond our ability to comprehend. To be candid, I am not a big fan of being in God's waiting room.

We are all waiting for something: a medical diagnosis, a paycheck to arrive, a promotion to be announced, a relationship to be restored, a prodigal to return, a heart to mend, a healing to occur. We're in the waiting room for the first time or the hundredth time. And we're here for a reason. Be still and listen intently to God today . . . He's getting ready to call your name. Keep praying. Keep connecting with other believers. He is up to something—and that's a promise!

Look back at your list of the thing(s) you are waiting on God for. Spend time before the Lord today asking Him to prepare your heart for His answer. Record anything He reveals to you below:

Look back at what He revealed to you at the end of Day 4. List a change in your life (your treatment plan) that you sense God is prompting you to make.

unexplainable change

PRAYER AND THE WORD

Please read aloud ACTS 1:15–26

Did you know that some psychologists suggest people can actually become addicted to being busy? That sounds so strange to me during this season of my life when I often feel like a hamster spinning in a wheel—taking care of my children's needs before, after, and sometimes during school; keeping my kitchen counter uncluttered enough to prepare dinner; remaining organized enough to keep the refrigerator and pantry stocked. Most days, life feels like a whirlwind with a never-ending to-do list and endless demands for my time and attention.

For three years the disciples traveled nonstop, watching Jesus and ministering alongside Him. They did their best to wrap their minds around His stories and teachings. The crowds had endlessly pressed in, demanding time and attention. The disciples were on their feet constantly with little or no time for rest. Even when Jesus took them away to teach them in private, it seemed as though *somebody* always found them.

Then He was crucified and they were flooded with grief. Three days later, He rose again and they were overtaken by joy and wonder. After His resurrection, more teaching followed, much of which they still didn't understand. On top of that, they were told not to concern themselves with an earthly kingdom. That must have thrown them for a loop. In their minds, the kingdom was the whole point! Finally, at His ascension, Jesus left them again and told them to return to Jerusalem and wait. Surely, those ten days were painstakingly long. The whole thing was confusing and mysterious. Sure, the Holy Spirit was going to come—but what did that really *mean*?

And so they continually prayed. They were desperate for God's direction. They were probably a little stir crazy, too. Nevertheless, there was still another task that needed to be completed before they were ready for what was going to happen next.

Read Acts 1:15–24. What did Peter insist the disciples needed to do?

What were the requirements for this position? See Acts 1:22.

In order to complete this task, what two resources did the disciples depend on?

Other important details we don't want to miss are in this passage of Scripture. First, there are no longer only twelve apostles and several women—the group of gathered believers has grown to about 120. Since Jesus' resurrection, the Christian church had already begun to multiply. Peter's choice of words in what they were going to be doing was also interesting.

Look carefully at Acts 1:17. What word does Peter use?

It appears that Peter has begun to make the connection—they are going to be servants of people, not kingdom rulers. Peter is beginning to understand that following Jesus is no longer a civic cause, a type of social reform, or a quest for political power. It is *ministry.*

How did Paul describe the ministry he was given to do in 2 Corinthians 5:17–21?

While Peter understood they were called to preach God's reconciliation of people to Himself, we'll see that he still has quite a way to go in understanding that God meant *all people*. Peter is a Jew and feels called to minister to the Jewish people. Peter knew that there needed to be twelve disciples, just as there were twelve tribes of Israel. In Jewish thought, the number twelve signifies "perfect administration."[4]

What else had Jesus told the disciples in Matthew 19:28 that necessitated choosing someone to take Judas's place?

Peter's leadership in choosing the twelfth disciple was taken directly from his knowledge of the Scriptures. In Acts 1:20 Peter quotes from Psalms 69 and 109, confident his audience was familiar with these references. Peter knew when he quoted these verses from the Psalms to the rest of the disciples that any one of them could likely recite the psalm in its entirety.

Look up 1 Peter 1:4, 12–21 and 2 Peter 2:1–3. Why is it so important that we be avid students of the Word of God?

It is important that we understand the use of this teaching style. As we get further into the story of Acts, we are going to see key players like Peter, Stephen, and Paul use references to the Old Testament in their sermons to the people of Israel. While we are reading only one verse on the pages of Acts, the hearers of the day were processing entire passages of Scripture when they heard the verse quoted. I hope this spurs within you a desire to take the time to read cross-references in Scripture while you are reading your Bible. If you don't, it is easy to misunderstand what is being taught.

Jot down the emotions expressed in Psalm 69. How might any of them apply to what Jesus was going through at the time of His trial and death? How could these same responses apply to the disciples during this time?

THE DISCIPLES' EMOTIONS

_____

_____

_____

_____

_____

_____

JESUS' EMOTIONS

_____

_____

_____

_____

_____

_____

What are some of the promises David speaks of at the end of Psalm 69? List them below:

A teaching method commonly used by the rabbis of Jesus' day was to quote a verse or passage of Scripture while telling a story. The rabbi depended on his audience's ability to determine the context from which the verse had been taken. Jesus used this teaching style often in His parables.

Before we close today, complete the following exercise:

What are some passages of Scripture you commonly recite in praying to God, encouraging your brothers and sisters in Christ, or in sharing your faith with others?

Here are some of my favorites:

Philippians 1:6
Ephesians 2:10
Ephesians 3:20–21
Colossians 3:1–4
Isaiah 43:1–3
Psalm 40

Write your favorites out on a piece of paper, or type them, print them, and stick them in your Bible study book. If you are completing this in a small group, make enough copies for all of your group members. If you are completing the study alone, write them out on notecards and place them around your home. Our knowledge of the Word of God is meant to be shared! Make a commitment to learn a new verse someone shared in your group or choose a verse we have covered thus far in this study and begin to commit it to memory.

See you tomorrow, dear one.

PRAYER AND THE WORD, CONTINUED

Please read aloud ACTS 1:15–26

Yesterday we discussed the teaching style wherewith the rabbis of Jesus' day quoted a verse from a passage of Scripture, knowing that their hearers understood the context of the verse in its entirety. Unfortunately, many of us today do not know the Scriptures to that extent. The consequences of this lack are sobering when we consider that Jesus used this teaching style often. When we don't realize the context from which Christ was quoting, we often miss profound and enriching insights from His teaching. Understanding Jesus' use of the Scripture (what we call the Old Testament, of course, was the Scripture the Jewish people had) gives us greater insight as to what was actually occurring in the hearts and minds of the people.

In Acts 1:20, Peter uses this method. Let's resume by looking at the second psalm quoted by Peter.

Read Psalm 109 in its entirety. What comfort could the disciples gain from this passage of Scripture regarding their current circumstances?

Have you ever made the connection that a person's knowledge of the Scriptures will directly impact their ability to be a minister of reconciliation? Why do you think that is so?

When I was in my early thirties, I signed up to be a part of the prayer team at my church. I had two small children and little time to commit to ministry outside my home. This opportunity, however, took place on Sunday mornings while I was already at church, and my children were tenderly cared for by the beautiful women in the church nursery.

I was paired up with two amazing ladies, Diane and Angie, and we prayed during the service. This ministry experience stirred within me a deep desire to become a student of the Word of God. When these women prayed, they spoke God's Word back to Him. They reminded Him of the promises He had made. They reiterated His miracles and believed in faith that He was still a God capable of mighty works. They aligned their hearts with His as they prayed the words that God spoke about His love and care for His people. These women knew the Scriptures, and their prayers were *powerful.* To be honest, I thought of myself as a pretty savvy Christian at this point in my life, but getting down on my knees next to these women made me aware of how much I still had to learn. I *desperately* wanted to know God in the way that they knew Him, and I knew that meant I needed to study and learn His Word.

What are some practical steps you can take to obtain a greater knowledge of the Word?

In the coming days of study, we will learn that without a thorough knowledge of the Word of God, the disciples and early believers could not fulfill their mission. We are also going to see how important they felt it was for new believers to be committed to their understanding of the Scriptures—especially non–Jewish converts who had no knowledge of the Old Testament. If you and I are going to live unexplainable lives that are led and directed by the Holy Spirit, we must be committed to knowing the truths presented in God's Word.

This isn't going to happen by allowing our spiritual growth to come solely through a daily devotional reading. It isn't going to happen by just attending church each Sunday and then leaving our Bible untouched on the nightstand the rest of the week. It isn't going to happen by setting aside a mere five minutes at the beginning of our day to read the Scriptures. It requires being intentional. It's going to take commitment. It's going to take a desire to study God's Word. This will require being focused about how we spend our time so we're not distracted every time our cellphone chimes or laptop dings. We need to be *serious* about knowing Jesus and becoming like Him. Because many of us do spin like hamsters in a wheel, it'll also require determination and accountability.

Here's the good news. You've already committed to study God's Word by working through this Bible study! Congratulations!

List below the name(s) of someone who can hold you accountable in carrying out that commitment.

Welcome to discipleship, my friend—a commitment to the study of God's Word and the practice of prayer. Let's dig a little deeper into this prayer aspect.

Read Acts 1:24–25.
What did the disciples ask of God and what about Him gave them confidence to do so?

One question I'm going to ask Jesus when I get to heaven is, "What exactly did you see in Matthias's heart that caused You to choose him?"

What do you think it may have been? Why?

Next, they did something that may sound strange to us: they cast lots. This isn't some kind of "eeny meeny miny moe" playground exercise. Casting lots was a legitimate practice in the lives of the Jews actually instituted by God. Back in Exodus when the Lord was giving directions to His people Israel on how to properly live, He instituted the use of the Urim and Thummim (Exodus 28:30). They served as an assurance that the high priest who wore them would receive perfect enlightenment as to the will of God in questions beyond human understanding. In this situation in Acts it meant being able to see the core of Matthias's and Justus's hearts. This was the method of casting lots, and its primary use was to discover God's will in various situations. Note that this is the only time we see the apostles use this practice.

As believers in Jesus, we rely on prayer and the Word of God to make our decisions. Through both we provide opportunity for the Holy Spirit to direct us. These are the two important ways we seek God's will and direction for our lives. These first-century disciples still did not have the Holy Spirit. He became the replacement for the Urim and Thummim because He is God living in us, guiding us into all truth. While we no longer need a Urim or Thummim, we often wonder, "What is God's will in this situation I am facing?"

This raises a vital point. When we constantly seek signs from God to declare His will for our lives, I believe this greatly grieves the Holy Spirit inside us. Essentially, it robs Him of His job of being our Counselor. Look how Jesus described the work of the Holy Spirit.

The Complete Jewish Bible[5] renders John 15:26 like this: "When the Counselor comes, whom I will send you from the Father—the Spirit of Truth, who keeps going out from the Father—he will testify on my behalf."

I love this translation because it tells us that the Holy Spirit continuously pours forth new knowledge. He continually guides us and directs us to align our heart with the heart of the Father! He is the communicator of God's will in our time of questioning.

Tomorrow, we are going to discover the Holy Spirit's magnificent debut into the lives of the early Christians, but before we close today, let's take some time for reflection. Consider this:

> I think a lot of us need to forget about "God's will for my life." God cares more about your response to the Spirit's leading **today, in this moment,** than about what we intend to do next year. In fact, the decisions we make next year will be **profoundly impacted by the degree to which we submit to the Spirit right now, in today's decisions** . . . it's much less demanding to think of God's will for your future than it is to ask Him what He wants you to do **in the next ten minutes.**[6] (emphasis in original)

Ask the Lord to examine your heart. Is it truly your deepest desire to know God intimately through His Word and prayer, or have you only invited His powerful Spirit into certain areas of your life?

What are one or two things you can do today to begin to increase the time you spend with God in His Word and in prayer, thus allowing the Holy Spirit to speak to you more clearly?

A POWERFUL PENTECOST

Please read aloud ACTS 2:1–8

Considering that Jesus' death occurred on the Jewish holiday of Passover and His resurrection on the Feast of Firstfruits, I'm sure the disciples began to hope that something significant was about to happen on Pentecost. After all, they had been stuck inside this "room" for ten days now! They had replaced Judas Iscariot with Matthias, solidifying the twelve apostles, and remained in prayer. As the sun set to usher in Pentecost, I am sure their emotions were running high! We know they followed Jesus' directions carefully because Luke tells us that when the Holy Spirit arrived, they were gathered in one place (Acts 2:1).

Read Acts 2:2–4.
What did the disciples hear?

What did they see?

What were they able to do?

The method of the Holy Spirit's arrival is deeply significant and a moment of recollection for the disciples. Every year on Pentecost the Jewish people read Ezekiel's vision and call.

Read Ezekiel 1:1–4 and record the similarities between Ezekiel's vision on Pentecost and what the disciples were now experiencing.

Now read Ezekiel 2:1–8 and record what God was calling Ezekiel to do as a result of this vision.

Let's picture the scene. The disciples were gathered together celebrating Pentecost. Most likely Peter is reading from Ezekiel aloud to them: "As I looked, behold, a stormy wind came out of the north . . ." and suddenly Philip shouts out, "Wait, did you guys hear something? Is there a storm kicking up?" Peter dismisses him and continues reading, "and a great cloud, with brightness around it, and fire flashing forth continually"! James and Andrew chime in, "No! Peter! Look! Flames of fire are approaching! Look up! Pay attention!" Thomas begins laughing and shaking his head. "Here we go again! Jesus is going to do something to totally freak me out!" (I'm not sure of the Aramaic translation for that.) Contemplative John observes the scene and announces, "Others heard that sound too, Philip. Look, they're coming this way!" Peter sits dumbfounded—it's Ezekiel's vision. It's happening before their eyes. Peter quickly scans through the rest of the text: "Son of man, I send you to the people of Israel, to nations of rebels, who have rebelled against me," and suddenly Peter is using a Coptic dialect, John is speaking Latin, and Andrew is speaking Greek. What is going on? All the other disciples are speaking in other languages, too. Peter knows they must act. He reads the next section of the text under his breath while trying to take in the scene at the same time. "And you shall speak my words to them, whether they hear or refuse to hear . . ."

God gave the disciples the Holy Spirit so they could speak to the people. We're told in Ezekiel 3:8–9 that God would strengthen the apostles to withstand any opposition they might face in their mission. Write out these verses below:

What command did God give to Ezekiel in Ezekiel 3:8–9 and thus now, to the disciples, by likening the Holy Spirit's arrival to this previous vision on Pentecost?

Ezekiel's vision also informs us of the tremendous responsibility that God was placing upon the apostles. What does God say in Ezekiel 3:17–21?

Here it is, in living color, brought to mind by the similarity of the wind and the fire—the apostles were the new watchmen of Israel. Though the Israelites quite possibly would not listen to them, the disciples were to warn them and show them the way to repentance through the Lord Jesus Christ. They were not to be afraid, for God promised to give them great resolve in communicating the fact of the resurrection. Now they understood why they were given the Holy Spirit! However, unlike Ezekiel who merely *experienced* the Holy Spirit, they were now *empowered* by the Spirit and therefore able to speak in other languages.

I always read this story and assumed the disciples were in somebody's upstairs attic because Luke says it occurred in the "house" where they were sitting. Because of some other details that he shares later, I believe this "house" refers to the Lord's house or the temple.

According to Acts 2:5, who else was in the "house" of the Lord with them?

Read Acts 2:6 carefully in the different versions below:

When they heard the loud noise, everyone came running, and they were bewildered to hear their own languages being spoken by the believers (NLT).

When this sound occurred, a crowd came together and was confused because each one heard them speaking in his own language (HCSB).

When this sound occurred, the crowd came together, and were bewildered because each one of them was hearing them speak in his own language (NASB).

There are three events happening very quickly in this verse. What are they?

The Jewish people who were there that day, as well as the disciples, knew about Ezekiel's vision and call. When they heard the mighty wind, they remembered. They knew that, unlike what they were witnessing, Ezekiel had spoken only in Hebrew.

Read Acts 2:7–8.
What questions did the onlookers ask?

I don't know about you, but this whole scene just gives me the chills! Think about how God instituted the migratory feast of Pentecost at Mt. Sinai over a thousand years before. God knew all along what He was ultimately going to do on the day of this feast for His people Israel and the world at large. He had begun to give them a glimpse of it through His prophet Ezekiel over six hundred years earlier, and now, on this historic day, the ultimate purpose of Pentecost was coming to pass!

What does Peter tell us about the Lord's timeline in 2 Peter 3:8–9?

Write out verse 9 here:

Could it be that Peter remembered this particular Pentecost when he penned that letter? I am reminded of a saying Jesus frequently repeated during His earthly teaching.

Look up the following passages and notice what commonalities you see: Matthew 11:15; 13:9, 43; Mark 4:9; Luke 8:8.

Write the common truth found in these verses here:

See Deeper Discoveries on the call and mission of the prophet Ezekiel at ericawiggenhorn.com.

Read aloud Ezekiel 36:24–27.

What other promise does God fulfill according to these verses? (See if you can find three of them fulfilled in the death and resurrection of Jesus and Acts' Pentecost.)

Remember, my friend, that God is not slow in keeping His promises as we may understand slowness. His timing is perfect! What is a promise of God that you need to cling to today? Is it that He loves you, or is always with you, or will never leave or forsake you? You can trust God to do what He has promised *every single time.* Maybe the Holy Spirit is prompting you to slow down and do some listening. Pray and ask the Lord for ears to hear! Confess to Him that you don't want to miss anything He is trying to tell you today, in this very moment. Pray and seek His answer and then write below anything He impresses on your heart:

WEEK 2 | DAY 4
A POWERFUL PENTECOST, CONTINUED

Please read aloud ACTS 2:1–41

Yesterday we read how Ezekiel's first vision and call from God were read aloud to the Jewish people on Pentecost. This answered a lot of questions for me. I hadn't understood how it was that the disciples frequently misunderstood what Jesus was saying to them, but then suddenly now, the Holy Spirit comes and they are instantly aware of what they must do. It almost makes the Holy Spirit's arrival seem like some sort of mystical hocus-pocus revelation. However, when we understand the connection with Ezekiel's vision, then we have some insight about their sudden comprehension! It was through illuminating the ancient promises given through the prophet Ezekiel that the disciples came to make sense of what was happening to them now.

This is important because we often hear people say, "The Lord told me such and such . . ." Listen, the Spirit speaks through the Word of God and enables us to apply it to our lives. If we truly want to be certain what we are sensing is from the Holy Spirit, we need to compare it with the principles and instructions given in Scripture. The disciples knew what to do because the Holy Spirit led them to the prophet Ezekiel and that was how He delivered their marching orders, not some random, unheard of idea out of left field. Everything we hear from the Spirit will *always* line up with Scripture.

What does this mean for us? If we want to truly be led by the Holy Spirit, we have to know the Word of God. I know I keep hammering home this same point, but I truly believe that one of the primary reasons we don't see or feel the Holy Spirit working in our lives is because we have not committed ourselves to knowing God through His Word. By neglecting the Bible, we not only grieve the Holy Spirit, we stifle His ability to speak to us. Look back at Week 1 Day 1 and see what you wrote for some of your examples/life experiences. *Those were times when the Holy Spirit was speaking to you.* Now here's another important reflection:

Share one of the most profound times the Holy Spirit spoke to you through His Word:

Take time to examine the life events and the timelines in which they occurred. Do you notice any patterns? Are there more times that are recent or were they mostly a long time ago? Did they mostly occur during a certain circumstance or season of your life?

If we notice the Spirit speaking less frequently rather than more often, what have you learned thus far in this study about how to better hear Him?

Let's get back to our story. We read yesterday that some Jews were inquisitive about what was happening at Pentecost. They knew it was something incredible. Jews from Africa, Europe, Asia, and the Middle East were all in town for the Jewish feast. The disciples were able to speak to all the people in their own individual tongues. While some marvel at this, others dismiss and mock the amazing event—and Peter is propelled into action!

Read what Peter did next in Acts 2:14–15.

Now look up Ezekiel 2:1 and write that verse here:

What similarities do you see?

Now beginning with verse 16 through 21, Peter quotes from the Old Testament prophet Joel to bring understanding to the people in regard to what they were witnessing.

> For Deeper Discoveries on the Feast of Pentecost and the prophet Joel go to ericawiggenhorn.com.

List some of the events included in Joel's prophecy in Acts 2:16–21. Put a star next to the ones that were being fulfilled right at that moment.

Read Acts 2:23–28.

Who did Peter suggest was really the catalyst behind Jesus' crucifixion?

Although God purposed for Him to be crucified, what else did God do on Jesus' behalf?

Peter quotes from Psalm 16 in Acts 2:25–28.

Preserve me, O God, for in you I take refuge.
I say to the Lord, "You are my Lord;
  I have no good apart from you."
As for the saints in the land, they are the excellent ones,
  in whom is all my delight.
The sorrows of those who run after another god shall multiply;
  their drink offerings of blood I will not pour out
  or take their names on my lips.
The Lord is my chosen portion and my cup;
  you hold my lot.
The lines have fallen for me in pleasant places;
  indeed, I have a beautiful inheritance.
I bless the Lord who gives me counsel;
  in the night also my heart instructs me.
I have set the Lord always before me;
  because he is at my right hand, I shall not be shaken.
Therefore my heart is glad, and my whole being rejoices;
  my flesh also dwells secure.
For you will not abandon my soul to Sheol,
  or let your holy one see corruption.
You make known to me the path of life;
  in your presence there is fullness of joy;
  at your right hand are pleasures forevermore.

How long did David set the Lord before him?

Why was David glad?

What does David say about the body of the Holy One?

Read Acts 2:29–36.
How does Peter explain what is happening?

In verse 34 Peter quotes Psalm 110:1. How do we know that David had to have been prophesying?

What two titles did Peter give Jesus in Acts 2:36?

Peter's use of Psalms 16 and 110 is significant. Jesus is not only the promised Messiah of Israel, He is also the rightful King and Lord over all of the earth. Israel was currently under Roman rule. Caesar was the rightful ruler in the mind of the Romans, and it was the Roman government that appointed the rulers of the temple. Peter's claim made some waves, to say the least. Consider this explanation as to the ripple effect of his statement.

> Peter has launched the early Christians on a double collision course with the authorities. Jesus is the true King, which means that his followers need no longer regard the current authorities as absolute. What is more, the authorities themselves were responsible, along with the pagans, for Jesus' death. Their power was called into question.[7]

Read Acts 2:37–39.
How did the people respond to Peter's sermon?

What did Peter tell them to do?

Who did he say was eligible to do so?

Please remember this important statement by Peter in verse 39, because we will see later in our study, that while Peter clearly stated it under the power and direction of the Holy Spirit, he did not fully understand it yet.

True repentance always leads to some sort of action. Peter's words demanded a response from them. What Peter said was devastating to a Jewish person of that day! Today, we often refer to the death and resurrection of Jesus as the "good news," but for the hearers of Peter's sermon, this was horrible news. They had waited their entire lives for God to finally send the Messiah. Rabbis, priests, and Pharisees spent countless hours poring through the Scriptures to try and determine His arrival. The Messiah was their hope for the spiritual and physical restoration of the nation of Israel—and they not only failed to recognize Him, they foolishly murdered Him! Their deeper question is, "What does this mean for the future of Israel? Are all of God's promises in regard to the Messiah now null and void?"

What did Peter call the current generation in Israel in Acts 2:40 and why? (See Matthew 23:33–36.)

How many heeded his message? See verse 41.

There were undoubtedly thousands of migratory Jews present for the festival. While we read of the three thousand and rejoice, the fact is many more rejected the message than received it.

What did Jesus say in Matthew 23:37?

Have you accepted the message? Has it led to repentance in your life? Maybe there is an area of your life in which the Holy Spirit is prompting you to take action. The good news of Christ demands a response.

Bow before the Lord today and ask Him for a heart to hear Him. Record anything He reveals to you below:

WEEK 2 | DAY 5
A POWERFUL RESPONSE

Please read aloud ACTS 2:42–47

Every Thursday morning at 8:00 a.m., I meet with a friend to pray. We pray for *the* church and for *our* church. We pray for revival and for the Christian church to function like the early church did in Acts 2:42–47. Before you begin to think I'm a spiritual rock star, let me tell you it was totally her idea. I went along with it, inspired by her story of two sisters, Peggy and Christine Smith, who decided to pray, and it led to revival in the Hebrides islands off Scotland's west coast.[8] My friend loves Jesus and she loves the women God places in her path. In fact, she loves them just like Jesus loves them—with her very life. She pours out every ounce of her heart and soul into doing everything she can to help them become more like Him. Because she knows the Word of God, she knows that prayer is the most important step for that transformation to happen.

We hear a lot of complaints today about the church. The world mocks it. Even Christians may disparage it. Wounded people shout from the rooftops why they left church and will never go back. But it seems we don't hear of many people who are praying for it—not nearly enough, anyway. The truth is that the description of the Christian church that we read about in Acts 2:42–47 is most likely a far cry from your church experience. You may have seen glimpses of it from time to time, but it may not be the everyday reality of what goes on inside your church.

I want you to think about my friend. She doesn't shake her fists, upset by the fact that Christians aren't living the way they are supposed to be. She bends her knees and invites others to do the same. She realizes it's not her job to rant on Facebook trying to convict them. It's her job—and yours and mine—to intercede for them and invite the Holy Spirit to have His way in their hearts. None of us are fully living the way the early church members did, but we can all move a step closer, and we start by praying.

Who could you meet with to pray for your church and the church? Get creative! Start a Facebook group, invite friends to log on at 8:00 a.m. every morning and pray your posted prayer for the day. Or ask your friends to take turns posting the prayer.

If you have regularly committed to a prayer time with other believers, can you share some of the ways God has answered you?

Why do you think prayer is the key to allowing the Holy Spirit to radically transform us and help us live unexplainable lives?

What I want you to grasp is not how remarkable it was that three thousand people responded to Peter's message that day. Anybody can walk to a pool and get baptized. What is remarkable about Peter's message is the *unexplainable lives* that were produced in response to the message.

Look carefully at Acts 2:42 and list four things these new believers committed to:

Let's break down these four activities and allow the Holy Spirit to do a heart check within us. *They devoted themselves to understanding the Word of God and the message of Christ.* Check. That's exactly the purpose of this Bible study. *They devoted themselves to engaging with other believers in the community.* Are you completing this

Bible study in a small group or church setting? Check. Encouraging and holding others accountable and being open to receiving those things from other members of the church is being "devoted to the fellowship." Are you completing this study all alone? Who could you invite to complete it with you? *The "breaking of bread" is the celebration of the sacrament of communion.* Jesus did this with His disciples the night before His arrest and commanded them to continue doing it in remembrance of Him. (See Luke 22:14–21.) When Jesus celebrated "communion" with His disciples, He was actually celebrating the Passover meal and explaining how He was the true Passover Lamb. It wasn't just the twelve apostles who were celebrating Passover that night; *it was every single God-fearing Jew on the face of the earth.*

I believe being devoted to "the breaking of bread" means being devoted to a local church body. Part of the remembrance is the acknowledgment that you are part of a celebration beyond yourself and your own personal relationship with Jesus Christ. You are only *one member of an entire kingdom* and you are meant to gather with other kingdom citizens and participate in this command of our King. And that, my friend, means your local church. *Last, but certainly not least, they were devoted to prayer.*

See Acts 2:43–47.

Now here's the cool part! What was the result of the believers' devotion? Write verse 43 here:

What does "filled with awe" mean to you in your own journey with Him right now?

What other unexplainable results occurred in this passage?

What happened daily in the lives of these early believers as stated in Acts 2:46–47?

What did God do as a result of this unity among them?

Take a look at John 17:20–23. What had Jesus prayed for these believers (and for you and me) the night before He went to the cross?

You may feel convicted while reading today's lesson. You may feel angry recalling how you were disappointed by someone in the church. (We'll address that later in this study.) But for today, I want you to do what my friend Jim often says: "Look in the mirror, not out the window!" Today it's about you and me. Are we brave enough to look inside our hearts and ask ourselves some tough questions? Hold my hand and take a deep breath. This might be a little painful. I know it was for me as I was typing it out.

How much time can you honestly say you devote to each of these activities?

In what specific ways are you devoted to other believers?

What sacrifices have you made, or are you willing to make, in order to be more committed in these four areas?

In what activities do you currently participate that make your commitment difficult to carry out? Are there any you can eliminate?

If you don't see a strong commitment to these four activities from your church leadership, what could you do? (Hint: reread the first paragraph in today's lesson.)

Do you intentionally take the time to make yourself aware of the needs of others within your local church and pray about how you could play a part in helping to meet them?

We're going to examine the economic structure of the early church more closely in the days ahead, but for now, when I say "needs," I don't want you to merely think of tangible things. It could mean keeping your eyes and ears open to someone who may need a word of encouragement. It could mean walking through your church doors while praying, "Lord, show me who needs me to pray with them today." He may lead you to an emotional or spiritual need just as readily as a physical one.

On Sunday, our children often complain that my husband and I talk too long after the service is over. They've been there all morning and they are hungry and ready for a change of scenery. Over and over again, Jonathan and I have quoted Jill Briscoe to them: "The ethos of this family is service to Jesus." When we go to church, we go to serve. When someone wants to talk with us or ask for prayer, we make ourselves available. Though we undoubtedly receive more from the fellowship of Sunday mornings than we ever give, that is not the reason we go. We're there to worship and to serve—to give of ourselves to God and to our fellow believers, trusting that God will give us all we need to serve Him well.

These questions are tough. Thank you for being courageous enough to really think them through. You are highly esteemed by your heavenly Father. Jesus is smiling, and the Holy Spirit is dancing with joy! I want you to notice, dear one, the benefit is not for them alone.

Describe below how the believers felt in Acts 2:43, 46.

Oh, that we can be filled with awe and have "glad and sincere hearts" as we meet together! If church has become mundane and feels like a burden, may we learn from the awe of these early believers. And may we remember, my friend, to bend our knees and hearts to pray.

unexplainable courage

A BEAUTIFUL ENCOUNTER

Please read aloud ACTS 3:1–7

The name of Jesus brings new life to the most hopeless of situations. The power of Jesus is worth more than anything money can buy. Today's story brings both these truths to life as a man who was lame from birth encounters the beautiful person of Christ.

Read Acts 3:1 carefully and record the following:

WHO:

WHAT:

WHERE:

WHEN:

WHY:

Now read Acts 3:2 carefully and record the following:

WHO:

WHAT:

WHERE:

WHEN:

WHY:

The first verse about Peter and John gives us much information. First of all, they were men of prayer. They could have reasoned that due to their knowledge of Christ, they no longer needed to pray. They had all the answers and knew more than the rabbis! However, they went to the temple to pray and worship God. They believed in the power of prayer. Second, they were men of faith. They did not carry out their religious convictions with placid regularity and indifference. Witnessing God miraculously answer prayers in the last three and a half years through Jesus had emboldened them. Since His death and resurrection, they witnessed their own miraculous answers to prayer as well. And they were men of the Word. The Jewish laws commanded them to pray, so pray they did. People of prayer, faith, and the Word. These are the people who are ready and available for God to use. And use them He did!

How about the third character in this story? What does he do in verse 3?

Peter did two things in response to this man in verse 4. List them both:

What did the man do in verse 5, and what was his motivation?

I can easily picture this scene in my mind's eye. The man probably had a jar sitting at the edge of his mat. Eyes cast down he repeatedly called, "Have mercy on me, I am lame!" "Can you spare some change?" "Please help me!" The monotony of his existence and the shame of his condition led him to repeat his cries despite disinterest in his hearers. Cutting himself off emotionally from those who passed by afforded him some shred of dignity. However, Peter refused to allow him to suffer humiliation. "Look at us!" Peter demanded.

Truthfully, when I encounter the homeless or others asking for help, I prefer not to look them in the eye. Vulnerability surfaces in both of us when our gaze meets. Eyes are a window to the soul, and I am forced to acknowledge that I am facing a person created by God, not a statistic. It is so much easier to look away. It's also easier for them. Rather than bear to see the scorn or shame in the eyes of a passerby, they look away in humiliation. While I wonder why Peter made the man look directly at him, I believe it was partly to communicate that he accepted him as he was. From gospel encounters with Jesus and His disciples, we know that some believed physical affliction could be a punishment for sin (see John 5:14, 9:2).

Don't you wonder what Peter saw as he gazed at the man? What exactly was Peter looking for? I imagine there were many other beggars scattered around the gate asking for alms, so I wonder why he chose to address this man in particular. The scene reminds me of another story in Scripture where Jesus chose to heal one particular man out of a multitude.

Read John 5:1–8 and record what Jesus asked the invalid:

How did the man answer Jesus?

How did Jesus respond?

Maybe what Peter was looking for was this man's "want to"—did he actually want to be healed? Truthfully, some people prefer to stay sick, whether physically, emotionally, or spiritually.

See Acts 3:6–7. What did Peter tell the man he did *not* have, and what *did* he have for him instead?

It is interesting how Peter throws in the tidbit about not having silver or gold.

What did we just read in Acts 2:45?

Was Peter lying? Of course not! The plight of the lame man could not be solved by silver or gold. Peter offered him a healing word, along with a healing touch. Peter graciously gave him the opportunity to exercise faith in Peter's words while he simultaneously extended an outstretched hand to the man. Peter stabilized him as he rose to his feet. What a beautiful picture of the love of Christ in action! It is one thing to share the healing power of the name of Jesus with someone in need. It is altogether wonderful to hold them up as they begin to walk in the power of it.

To whom are you willing to extend your right hand?

What circumstances, qualifications, or characteristics are you looking for before you decide to stop and extend it?

Scripture doesn't tell us exactly why Peter and John stopped to heal this particular man. It does imply that there was something they saw within him that prompted them to do so. Maybe the lesson for us consists of taking the time to engage with those in need around us. It takes courage to stop and look a vulnerable person directly in the eye. It's difficult to intently search another human's soul and then callously walk away. Could it be that if we truly asked God what to give them in the moment, He would reveal it to us by His Spirit?

What does 1 Corinthians 2:9–11 tell us?

If we were brave enough to gaze on the soul of another human being, no matter how corrupt the flesh that housed it might be, wouldn't that be pretty unexplainable apart from the prompting of the Holy Spirit?

WEEK 3 | DAY 2
A COMPLETE HEALING
Please read aloud ACTS 3:1–26

I have always been a sucker for a happy ending. I think most of us are. It's probably why Disney movies soar in popularity: the bad guy always gets his just deserts, the good guy always comes out on top, and the people who suffer live in the eternal bliss of happily ever after. Somehow no matter how hopeless the plot seems, we expect it to turn out right in the end. Well, Peter throws a horrific plot twist at his Jewish brothers as this story unfolds.

Read Acts 3:8–11.
Describe the reaction of the people in the temple.

What did the people do in verse 11?

Look at John 10:22–29, 37–38. What else had happened in this same location within the temple less than a year before?

From whom did Jesus claim the power to perform miracles?

From whom did Peter claim he had received the power to heal the lame man? See Acts 3:12–13.

What is the horrible plot twist that Peter throws in?

It gets even worse. What else does Peter say?

Finish Acts 3:15 according to your translation: "you killed the Author of life _____ _____ raised from the dead."

Don't you just love God's ways? "You blew it, guys! You messed up big time!" **But God.** You destroyed, God brought to life. Man's biggest mistakes can never thwart God's plans. The most wicked of men are no match for the goodness of God. You can never one-up the One who holds all of life in His hands.

According to Acts 3:16, how exactly was this man healed?

From where does the man's faith come?

What word does Peter use to describe the man's healing?

Peter is stating a couple of things. First, it is through the power of Jesus' name that the healing occurred. Second, it is Jesus Himself who grants us the faith to believe in His name. Finally, Jesus heals perfectly and completely. Every positive thing that happens then is granted by God.

What does James 1:17 tell us? Write the verse here:

Jesus' name healed this man physically and spiritually. We see him praising God and giving Him the glory for what had happened to him (v. 8). We also see him hanging on to Peter and John (v. 11) as the people drew near. I believe he was also emotionally healed. Peter possibly was the first person to address his needs without shaming him in the process or expecting something in return. This man felt safe with Peter and John. He trusted them. He knew they rejoiced in the healing work of Jesus right along with him. A perfect healing.

So often we want to offer people spiritual healing in Jesus' name, but we're un-willing to do the hard work of helping them experience healing emotionally or physically. We don't feel we have the strength to allow someone to "hold on to us" until they feel safe enough to venture out on their own. We speak the name of Jesus over them and then leave them alone to figure it all out. This man needed the emotional support of Peter and John to understand all that Jesus had done for him. They readily offered it to him.

Have you ever had an experience where people offered you spiritual support but you still left feeling emotionally bankrupt?

Why is it important to meet emotional and physical needs along with spiritual ones?

What else does James tell us in James 2:14–17?

After the appalling plot twist, however, Peter begins to usher them toward the happy ending.

What does Peter say about the actions of his Jewish brothers in Acts 3:17?

Peter wasn't merely giving them an out for crucifying Jesus. He was granting them hope for the future. According to Jewish law, atonement was offered for unintentional sins. Willful sins were another matter. Peter is saying, "Listen, there is a way out of this mess—don't lose hope!"

Read Acts 3:18–19.
What else does Peter tell them?

He gives them even more good news in verse 20. Who will come back again?

According to verse 21, when will this occur?

Which prophets did Peter mention who foretold of Jesus' suffering? See verses 22–25 and list as many as you can find.

For what specific reasons did God send Jesus to the people of Israel according to Acts 3:26?

Peter proclaims, "Listen everyone! There is a happily ever after—it's found in Jesus! Look at the blessing poured out on this man before your very eyes—perfect healing! Jesus is even greater than you understood the Messiah to be! You thought the Messiah would bring physical restoration to Israel, but Jesus brings physical, emotional, and spiritual restoration. He is a deliverer like Moses, a priest like Samuel, a fulfillment of covenant promise like Abraham. He is more than you imagined!"

List as many characteristics of Christ as you can from Colossians 1:15–20.

Christ came to do far more abundantly than we could ask or imagine (Ephesians 3:20). Have we missed aspects of Jesus' power or person in areas of our lives? Maybe the reason we don't feel compelled to meet physical and emotional needs in the lives of others is because we have not allowed Jesus to meet them in our own life. We have looked to God for spiritual healing to take us to heaven but have believed Him for little else. We may not miraculously walk, but a willingness to venture to new places with the help of others would be pretty unexplainable. We may still need to be under the care of a physician, but a willingness to accept our circumstance with trust would leave a whole lot of people baffled. The ability to forgive and be set free emotionally would astonish those who see and know what we've suffered.

Choosing to praise God rather than stay stuck in self-pity would inspire awe in those who know how we have been wronged. Jesus is big enough to bring those areas of refreshing in our lives. And when He comes again, He will restore all things.

What would your unexplainable, perfect healing look like?

MORE THAN A NAME

Please read aloud ACTS 4:1–8

Yesterday we read of the second miracle performed by the apostles. First they spoke in other languages, sharing the gospel message with their Jewish brothers visiting from all over the world in the temple at Pentecost. Now Peter, along with John, healed a lame man at the temple gate called Beautiful.

Look back at Acts 3:16 and list the two things that healed this man, according to Peter:

Right in the middle of Peter's explanation of the healing of the lame man another group of men turns up.

List the three people/groups of people who arrived on the scene in Acts 4:1:

How does Luke describe the emotional state of these people in verse 2?

Why do they feel that way?

We could call this collection of people the "establishment." They were the men in charge, the ones who held the authority within the temple. Both the captain of the temple guard and the chief priest were appointed by the Roman government. It was their job to maintain order and to squelch any form of insurrection or rioting.

The Sadducees did not believe in the resurrection of the dead. They were the religious "statesmen" who had been granted power to maintain control over the uneducated masses, so they rationally explained away the miracles of the Torah and discounted all other Jewish miracle stories as folklore. They were Israel's pragmatic elite.

What did they do to Peter and John in verse 3?

How did the people in the temple respond to Peter's message in verse 4?

No matter what the religious leaders did, they just couldn't stop the spread of the name of Jesus! We now see another two thousand men coming to faith in Jesus Christ and believing the message of the gospel. A visible testimony exudes unexplainable power. The people had witnessed a lame man walking. We can rationalize theological arguments, we can explain away prophecy as coincidence, but a broken life made whole before our very eyes is unexplainable. There is no argument for that. All a person can do is either praise God for what they see standing before them or walk away in stubborn disbelief.

What is one of the most remarkable testimonies you have heard someone share?

These religious leaders are in a conundrum. They want Peter and John to go away, stop talking about Jesus, and definitely cease mentioning resurrection. However, the disciples continue to show up in the temple insisting that Jesus has risen from the dead. The chilling words of Caiaphas spoken less than two months before about Jesus must have been echoing in their minds as they left the temple that night.

Look back at John 11:47–52. Record Caiaphas's words below.

How does John explain these words?

These religious leaders crucified Jesus as planned, but their problems only multiplied. Instead of having to try and explain away a miracle worker, they now were faced with the disciples' insistence on His resurrection!

What question did they ask Peter and John the following day? Refer to Acts 4:5–7.

Here we see Peter and John standing before the Sanhedrin, basically the same tribunal their Savior stood before less than two months before. Picture two men from a small rural town with little to no formal education appearing before the Senate in Washington, DC, and you'll get the idea. The religious leaders wanted to convene before Peter and John to intimidate them. They also wanted to trap them.

What warning did Moses give to the people of Israel in Deuteronomy 13:1–4?

What did Moses say in verse 5 should be done in such instances?

Interestingly, these religious leaders tried this same strategy with Jesus, and the event is reported in three Gospel accounts (Matthew 21:23, Mark 11:27, Luke 20:1).

Read Luke 20:1–8 and record what happened:

Let's not forget that Peter and John were standing right alongside Jesus when this had occurred. In fact, it probably brought a déjà vu to their minds and a chuckle to their lips at the irony of it. They were probably thinking, "So we're going to play this game again, huh, guys?"

See Acts 4:8–10.

How does this passage describe Peter?

How does Peter's answer refute the charge of Deuteronomy 13:1–4?

I get the biggest kick out of Peter sometimes. Here he is, a fishermen standing before the aristocrats saying, "Seriously, you are putting us on trial for showing kindness to a lame man? Don't you have anything better to do with your time?" Then Peter pulls no punches. "You guys asked, I'm going to tell you: Jesus of Nazareth. He is the name and the power. He came from God and God raised Him from the dead. Period."

There is no argument for a changed life. Many deny Jesus and His power or try to explain it away, but for the Sanhedrin, the problem of the Jesus followers only multiplied.

What has Jesus done in your life that just can't be explained?

Who have you told?

WEEK 3 | DAY 4

ORDINARY MEN, EXTRAORDINARY GOD

Please read aloud ACTS 4:1–22

The verse I pray will be cemented within your heart and mind from today's lesson is Acts 4:20. Please write it here:

About fifty days prior to these events, Peter had emphatically denied even knowing Jesus. Now he boldly stands in front of the Jewish High Court insinuating the foolishness of their questions. Fifty days and the filling of the Holy Spirit can transform a life.

We left yesterday in the middle of Peter and John's exciting court case. Standing before the Sanhedrin, Peter boldly declares that the name and power of Jesus healed the lame man. Not only do we witness a transformation in Peter's courage, we notice his ability to clearly present Christ to his audience. This same impetuous Peter, who often spoke without thinking and was rebuked by Jesus as a result, now eloquently defends his message. A humble fisherman stands debating with Israel's elite.

How does Peter describe Jesus in Acts 4:11?

What else does Peter boldly declare in the next verse? Write it here:

Peter is bringing to mind a time the religious leaders tried to trap Jesus in His teaching. We read this yesterday in Luke 20:1–8. Right after they questioned Jesus about His power and authority, Jesus told them a parable.

Read Luke 20:9–19 and identify the warning Jesus had issued to the religious leaders in telling this story:

What had been their reaction to the story?

Why did they not arrest Jesus then and there?

You had better believe these religious leaders had not forgotten this whole exchange between themselves and Jesus. They had been openly humiliated by this wandering, itinerant teacher. Now one of His followers stands before them throwing it back in their face. They must have been livid! However, just as in Luke's account with Jesus, their hands were tied.

When Jesus told this parable to the religious leaders, He too recalled a passage from the Jewish Scriptures.

Read Psalm 118:19–29 and record which verse Jesus quoted in Luke 20:9–19 below:

Restate Psalm 118:22 here:

Write the verse as it appears in Luke 20:17:

This psalm holds great significance in the daily life of the Jewish people. It is the culmination of six psalms (113–118) called the Hallel, meaning "praise." These psalms are always recited on Passover, the Feast of Tabernacles, and—you guessed it—Pentecost. They are also prayed at the beginning of each new month or when God would provide an unexpected blessing such as additional rain for their crops. Due to frequent recitation of these prayers, every Jewish person would be very familiar with them.

The Jewish people also shared a legendary tale that occurred during the construction of Solomon's temple. It was believed that the quarried stones for the construction of the temple had all been the same size and shape. One day they came across a different sized stone. The builders reasoned that the stone had been sent by mistake, so they rolled it over the cliff into the Kidron Valley. At the end of seven years, the construction was nearly completed and the builders requested the chief cornerstone to be sent. This reply came: "You must have it. We sent it to you a long time ago!" None of the remaining stones fit, for they were all the wrong size. Finally, one particular workman remembered rolling the odd-shaped stone over the cliff several years prior. They headed down to the Kidron Valley in search of the misshapen stone they had rejected, found it, and laboriously dragged it back up the cliff. The stone they had earlier rejected fit perfectly.[9]

What did Jesus say in John 2:19–22, and how did the disciples interpret what He had meant?

Peter makes it exceedingly clear to his audience that he is not preaching another god. Jesus is the fulfillment of Psalm 118.

How is He a picture of Psalm 118:22–24?

The Holy Spirit has illuminated these age-old prayers to Peter and John, bringing them to completion in Jesus Christ. Everything makes perfect sense to them. No wonder they were so bold and full of faith!

Read Acts 4:13 and list the adjectives the Sanhedrin uses to describe Peter and John:

I love how Luke tells us they had "been with Jesus." There is no amount of education that can replace that. We can know all about Jesus. We can study every word He's ever said and every miracle He's ever performed. We can listen to a thousand sermons, but until you sit at His feet and ask Him to teach you through His Holy Spirit, you're just an unschooled, ordinary person.

Look carefully at Acts 4:13 again. What word describes the members of the Sanhedrin in response to Peter and John?

Do you believe God could do something astonishing or amazing in your life during this fifty-day study, should you decide to allow the Holy Spirit to teach you?

What are you praying it might be? Healing a fractured marriage? Reconciliation of a broken relationship? Victory over a particular temptation? Development of a healthy habit? Peace with a difficult circumstance? Boldness to share the hope that is in you with a seeking friend or family member? Other? You may want to write your thoughts below.

Nothing in Peter's circumstances had changed during the last fifty days. What changed was his understanding and perspective. His priorities shifted. His focus sharpened. His purpose paved a mission that he relentlessly pursued. His whole sense of reality expanded and Jesus' resurrection became his abiding reality. Circumstances became inconsequential, resulting in Peter's becoming filled with courage and faith and the urgency to tell others about Jesus. Maybe the most unexplainable thing in our lives wouldn't be changed circumstances, but a change *in us*. As we allow the Holy Spirit to change us, the way we handle circumstances is bound to change as well, because our perspective toward them and our reaction to them will be different. By the power of the Holy Spirit we are able to walk through those circumstances with a confidence, peace, or joy that becomes unexplainable apart from God to those who are watching us.

And as we allow the Holy Spirit to fill us with His peace, joy, and confidence in God's goodness, our enemy's hands become tied. When we submit to Jesus, the enemy loses control. Just as in the account in Luke 20, the religious leaders feared that arresting Jesus would incite the crowds. These same religious leaders stood before Peter and John unable to do anything.

Read Acts 4:14–22.

How does Luke describe their problem?

What plan did they concoct?

How effective was this plan?

Though Peter is calling them ignorant fools, incapable of recognizing the work of God before their very eyes, Peter and John walk away unharmed.

Remember that this is the same Peter who waited outside when Jesus had stood in front of these same men less than two months before. Too afraid to enter and be identified as a follower of Jesus, he hid outside by the fire waiting to hear the verdict while denying Him when a servant girl asked (Luke 22:54–57). Here is a man now utterly transformed by the power of the Holy Spirit, changed by grace.

Will you continue to stand outside waiting to see what Jesus will do with someone else? Or will you sit at His feet and allow Him to change you into someone unexplainable apart from His power?

The decision is yours. Step by step. Day by day . . . continue this study and see what He may do . . .

WEEK 3 | DAY 5
BOLD PRAYERS, BIG RESULTS
Please read aloud ACTS 4:23–37

Again, we're going to begin today with a key verse I'd like you to remember. Write out Acts 4:31:

Think about the last time you received some really good news. Who was the first person you wanted to tell? I would venture to say it was the person you love most in the world and a person you know loves you. It could have been the person whom the news would most greatly affect, but by and large, the people with whom we celebrate are those we love dearly. When Peter and John were released by the Sanhedrin, they couldn't wait to share all that had happened with the rest of the believers!

How did their fellow believers respond to Peter and John's news in Acts 4:23–24?

What brings us joy when we've shared good news with others? Their response is to praise the Lord in prayer! These believers did not just start spouting off random phrases of praise. This prayer consists of very specific elements that I believe are worth emulating! In fact, I would suggest the components of their prayer are integral to the preparation for any type of ministry we seek to carry out in the name of Jesus.

"... Sovereign Lord, who made the heaven and the earth and the sea and everything in them, who through the mouth of our father David, your servant, said by the Holy Spirit,

"'Why did the Gentiles rage,
   and the peoples plot in vain?
The kings of the earth set themselves,
   and the rulers were gathered together,
   against the Lord and against his Anointed'—
for truly in this city there were gathered together
   against your holy servant Jesus, whom you anointed, both Herod and Pontius Pilate, along with the Gentiles and the peoples of Israel, to do whatever your hand and your plan had predestined to take place. And now, Lord, look upon their threats and grant to your servants to continue to speak your word with all boldness, while you stretch out your hand to heal, and signs and wonders are performed through the name of your holy servant Jesus." (Acts 4:24–30)

Let's break down this prayer together.

Carefully read Acts 4:24–30.
What did the believers first acknowledge in their prayer?

What did they imply about the role of the Holy Spirit in the Word of God?

What do they imply about the deeds of all people?

What did they ask the Lord to do?

Why do you think they specifically asked God to do that?

Deeper Discoveries about Psalm 2, which is quoted in Acts 4:23–27, can be found at ericawiggenhorn.com.

To be honest, I generally come to God in prayer predominantly asking for personal things that directly affect my life or the lives of those I love. I don't think there is anything wrong with that, since God tells us to bring our concerns before Him (1 Peter 5:7). However, when bringing a potential work or ministry before the Lord, I think the order of this prayer is crucial.

They start by acknowledging God's sovereignty.

Then they acknowledge that the Word of God is spoken through men inspired by the Holy Spirit.

Beyond that they acknowledge that every man on the face of the earth is carrying out God's will, whether they are aware of it or not.

Even people who do evil are under God's control. What a wonderful reminder when we see evil swarming around us and feel helpless to make a difference!

Not until the believers had fully acknowledged God's greatness, power, and purpose did they proceed to ask something from Him.

Why do you think acknowledging all these attributes of God in prayer would be important before undertaking any work in His Name?

Read Jesus' instructions on how to pray in Matthew 6:9–13 and record any similarities you find in the ordering of the elements of prayer.

When Jesus taught His disciples to pray, He emulated the priority of these prayer elements. He began by acknowledging God's perfection and sovereignty over the earth. He also emphasized praying for God's will, which is already being done in heaven, to be done on the earth. Jesus finishes the prayer with personal petitions, only after acknowledging the greatness and character of God and reminding themselves He had a purpose He was carrying out on earth.

Look at Matthew 6:8. What does Jesus say God knows?

Read Acts 4:29 carefully. What do you think the believers are really asking when they tell God to "consider their threats" or "take note of them" (NASB)?

We too must pray for boldness. We must also pray for God to manifest His power of protection over those who are boldly speaking in His name! Remember, it was the display of God's power that had confounded their accusers.

How would God answering their three specific requests in Acts 4:29 result in Jesus' name being exalted and the gospel message being spread?

for God to take note of their threats (i.e., intervene on the believers' behalf):

to continue to speak the Word with boldness:

for God to continue to grant them the power to perform miracles:

See Acts 4:31–33. How did God answer their prayer?

What was the result of their being filled with the Holy Spirit?

Oh, do we ever have a merciful God who knows how prone we are to fear! In His great mercy, He gave the disciples a physical manifestation of Himself in response to their prayer. Not only did the place where they were meeting shake, but they all became filled with the Holy Spirit.

What does Paul tell us in Galatians 5:25?

If we want to know if we're in step with the Spirit, this account gives us some clear things to ask ourselves. When these early believers were filled with the Holy Spirit their lives were marked by courage, unity, generosity, and power!

On a scale of 1 to 10, how would you rank yourself in these areas?

COURAGE	1	2	3	4	5	6	7	8	9	10
UNITY	1	2	3	4	5	6	7	8	9	10
GENEROSITY	1	2	3	4	5	6	7	8	9	10
POWER	1	2	3	4	5	6	7	8	9	10

Let's challenge ourselves to gather with other believers and ask God to enable us to speak with great boldness! Let's believe we serve the same God who stretched out His hand to heal and perform miraculous signs and wonders through the name of Jesus!

Who could you gather with this week to specifically pray for more boldness in your faith?

I've noticed in my own life a strong correlation between my scores in the chart and my prayer life. Perhaps there is in yours too. Today's story convicted me. I've realized something about my prayers: they're way too small for how big my God is. They're also way too self-focused. These early believers were much more concerned about Jesus' name being exalted and the message of salvation spreading than they were with having their individual needs met.

Again, praying for our individual needs is important; after all, Jesus taught His disciples to pray for their needs in Matthew 6. If we want an unexplainable life though, we've got to pray both for our daily bread and for power. We've got to pray for God's hand to be stretched out, not for a tiny tap of His finger! We have got to pray for His mission to be fulfilled: making disciples of all nations. We've got to remember that He has a sovereign plan that includes all people for all eternity.

What change is the Holy Spirit prompting you to make in your prayer life?

Is there a particular area of your life where you are "marching to the beat of your own drum" and you've fallen out of step with the Spirit?

When I was in high school, I played in the marching band. For hours we would march up and down the riverbed practicing our formations. As we shifted with the changing beats, having just one person off a step could potentially ruin the entire formation. A flute would crash into a tuba or a drummer would drop her stick. It required lots and lots of practice to get it right. And it often required practicing one part of the formation over and over again until we were ready to move on to the next segment. So it is with our spiritual formation.

Sometimes there is one little piece of our lives that is throwing the whole thing off, but just as with our band formations, we've got to keep at it. Often before we went out to the field to actually march, our director would talk us through the steps and warn us ahead of time where we would be most prone to mess up. So it is with our spiritual formation: prayer is where we talk it through. The Word is where our spiritual warnings are given. Keeping in step with the Spirit requires diligence and perseverance, but when you have it down, your life becomes a beautiful display accompanied by a skillful melody—it becomes unexplainably harmonious!

What changes do you need to make to improve your "spiritual formation"?

Here's some really good news, my friend. God answers prayer. God answers bold prayers with big results. Spend some time talking with Him today.

unexplainable mission

GRACE UPON GRACE

The bold prayers of the apostles at the end of Acts 4 produced big results. Up to this point Jesus and the Holy Spirit have been our primary protagonists, and the plot has been glorious! Acts 5 shifts scenes, highlighting the works and reactions of man. I doubt you even need to read the first few verses to realize that trouble is on the horizon. Before shifting into this next phase of the history of the church, we are reminded of the power of prayer. As we open up a new chapter of Acts, it is fitting to pause and reflect on this power that is available to us as believers in Christ. It is also important to carefully examine how our enemy uses people both inside and outside the church to come against it.

"And you call yourself a Christian?! I can't believe it!" I read statements like these on social media daily from one Christian to another. From the beginning of the early church, our enemy has engaged the same four tactics. It's time to fight back. How do we fight? We uncover our enemy's schemes and we fight back with prayer and the Word of God! Let's preview some of his tactics that we will discover in the remaining chapters of Acts and begin to pray *now*.

FEAR AND INTIMIDATION

In Acts 4, the fearless apostles boldly preached the name of Jesus, despite threats and intimidation. The Word of God quickly spread as the believers steadfastly prayed for boldness. When we propagate fear of "what ifs" across our social media portals, rather than pray for boldness, we play right into our enemy's hands.

What are some current fears you have seen propagated across social media? Circle those you have encountered:

TERRORISM   ECONOMIC INSTABILITY   RELIGIOUS PERSECUTION

MORAL INSURGENCE   EROSION OF RELIGIOUS LIBERTIES   OTHER: _____

What are some practical ways we can speak to those fears without disparaging other Christians?

COMPARISON

The church exploded and included various Jewish sects. In Acts 5, we will soon discover how comparison ensued and arguments erupted. The apostles, however, remained focused on their most important mission: the spread of the gospel. Then they prayed for direction and brought the factions together in prayer. Do our words on social media promote unity and invite others to pray with us, or do they criticize and divide?

What might be some creative ways to use social media as a platform for prayer?

I TELL YOU THE TRUTH . . .

It can be difficult to hear Jesus with so much noise surrounding us. Everyone has something to say. Paul opposed Peter face to face, using the Scriptures. Confronting believers' responses to current events, political agendas, or other areas of praxis is a private matter. Publicly disparaging our brothers and sisters delights our enemy. When we arrive in Acts 10, we'll see how it took dovetailed visions, an angelic messenger, and the Holy Spirit to change Peter's mind about the Gentiles. And this is Peter—the dynamic leader of the early church! We must give grace, not opinions. Only the Holy Spirit holds the power to change hearts, not our personal rhetoric.

If the Holy Spirit is the only One who can truly change hearts, then why is prayer especially important?

What might be alternative platforms to exhort believers other than social media?

CULTURE

Jesus' last command before ascending to heaven included taking the gospel to the entire world. It took several years, however, before Peter first witnessed to a Gentile. These men were sold-out for Jesus. They risked their lives for His kingdom, but their cultural and religious traditions continued to blind them (though we need to take into account their diligent upbringing in the Mosaic law).

How can we guard ourselves from becoming blinded by cultural bias or our religious traditions?

How then shall we live? God gave us a clear action plan in the book of Acts. Just as the early church did, you and I are going to face opposition. We have a real enemy whose desire is to destroy our churches corporately and our testimony individually. He wants to silence us. If he can't keep us quiet, then he wants what comes out of our mouths to serve his purposes rather than God's purposes. Scripture warns us that the closer we get to Christ's return, the harder Satan is going to work. So we need to be ready and wise.

We pray and challenge others to do the same.

We raise awareness of the enemy's tactics.

We teach the Word of God.

We trust the Holy Spirit to guide us.

It's war, but the victory is already ours!

This lifestyle of consistent gathering for prayer and the teaching of the Word of God by the early believers, along with the work of the Holy Spirit, enabled the apostles to preach the gospel powerfully. As they stood in the temple courts and the market squares preaching Christ crucified and risen, they knew they were not alone. They had the prayerful support of the rest of the believers behind them causing them to travel full speed ahead as they shared the gospel. They were united in mission and purpose, with nothing more important to them than the spread of the good news and their care for one another. We will also see how other believers became led and directed by the Holy Spirit to go out and do great things as well. The entire church body from top to bottom flourished as a result.

The lifestyle of the early believers demonstrated generosity with both their time and their resources. They met together daily and shared their lives. They gathered in prayer, focusing on their mission to tell others about Jesus. They practiced hospitality and devoted themselves to learning and knowing the Scriptures. The Holy Spirit manifested Himself powerfully among them. He protected His church and continued to advance. Let's invite Him to do the same in our day.

To learn more about giving, check out Deeper Discoveries at ericawiggenhorn.com.

WEEK 4 | DAY 2
A LITTLE WHITE LIE
Please read aloud ACTS 5:1–11

'm not going to sugarcoat it—today's teaching may be a little tough. Let's face it, when we start talking about lies, we're talking about the person and work of our enemy: the father of lies. Whenever he is brought into the equation, the math gets messy. And so it is today. In Acts chapter 4, we met Barnabas, called the Encourager. He willingly sold a piece of property he owned and presented the money for the care of those in need. Today we meet another man who did the same—sort of.

Read Acts 5:1–6.
Who are the husband and wife duo in this passage, and what did they do?

What does Luke make emphatically clear about Sapphira?

Who did Ananias lie to?

Who had caused him to lie?

Had Ananias been compelled to give all the money to the apostles?

What happened to Ananias as a result?

How did the rest of the believers respond?

Peter was not upset that Ananias had kept back part of the proceeds from the sale of his land. The sin was that Ananias lied about it. He presented the money to Peter as if it were all he had received. He was building up a spiritual image of himself that was false, purporting a level of generosity that was a sham. And he died in his deception.

Anytime we are tempted to lie or be untruthful, we have fallen into the enemy's snare.

When our actions are motivated by the applause and praise of other people over obedience to God, we are held in the enemy's clutches. I love how Matthew Henry states it: "Nothing can be more absurd than to hearken unto weak and fallible men more than unto a God that is infinitely wise and holy."[10] When our decisions are made based on a fear of what others might think of us or a desire to earn someone else's approval, we're walking a dangerous path.

This is a sobering story. Are we deceived about our own generosity? Luke tells this story immediately after the incredible power and grace that God bestowed on the generous believers. Now in contrast, death is introduced as a result of deception and greed.

Even more sobering, the deception continues.

See Acts 5:7–10. What happens in this passage?

Having been in women's ministry for nearly twenty years, I have often witnessed a common deception used by our enemy. Some women feel that a respectful wife must cover her husband's sin, falsely supposing that asking for help in dealing with a repeated pattern of sin in their home equals betrayal. A woman may find ways to rationalize, justify, and cover up sin, or even blame herself for her husband's involvement in something wrong. And in the end it results in death of their family unity and spiritual vibrancy.

I want to be clear: I'm not talking about "tattling" because your guy is insensitive at times. I'm not giving anyone a green light to sit around at Bible study and rail on her husband. I am talking about consistent, habitual, grievous sin: pornography, adultery, addiction, abuse, a double-life outside the church walls. I also want to be clear about this: *Your husband's sin is not your fault.* That fact doesn't make you sinless. It doesn't mean you are justified to do sinful things in response. It doesn't mean you lack responsibility in helping to bring reconciliation. You have made a covenant commitment to your husband. Seeking his best is what you stood at the altar and promised to do before God and witnesses. Helping him remain stuck in a cycle of sin is not helping him—it is breaking your own covenant you made before God.

So what is your responsibility? Sapphira had the opportunity to tell a trusted person in spiritual authority the truth about Ananias. Peter, of all men, understood grace. God, in His mercy, gave her the opportunity to come clean, but instead, she continued with the deception, either from her own sinfulness or a misguided loyalty to cover her husband's. And for this she lost her life. If you have this type of sin occurring in your home, your responsibility is to *get help.* God is calling you to bring the sin into the light by seeking the aid of a trusted pastor, counselor, or other mature Christian who can give you spiritual wisdom and guide you to resources you need to bring healing into the situation. When you continue to lie about its existence, then you also are leading a double life.

What does Paul tell us in 2 Corinthians 4:2?

What does James tell us about confession of sin and prayer? See James 5:16.

Again, bringing your husband's sin to light and asking for help doesn't mean blasting it on Facebook or announcing it openly in front of your whole church. It means going to a trusted spiritual authority, letting them know what is happening. It means being a woman of truth and grace. It requires examining the motivation behind the telling: Are you sharing your husband's sin so he is punished, or are you telling the truth so that by God's grace, he might be restored?

Consider too, that when you are conflicted spiritually, depleted emotionally, and possibly even suffering physically, you are especially prone to spiritual attacks. Time and again I have witnessed women in these situations suffering quietly until they eventually break. They fall prey to the enemy's schemes and head down their own destructive path, wreaking even more havoc on an already fractured family. Their home implodes and they are left among the ashes wondering what happened. Inviting other believers into your struggle guards you from making things worse by falling into temptation yourself.

The enemy's power primarily resides in the shadows and the darkness. When his schemes are brought into the light, his power becomes stripped from him. When you are the only one who knows about a situation, he has full power and control over the sin in your home. But when others are praying for you, encouraging you, and pointing you toward truth, the emotional and spiritual devastation begins to be combatted.

What resulted from the deaths of Ananias and Sapphira? See Acts 5:11.

We can keep trying to cover the sin and we may successfully take it to our grave, but we will have died doing it. Today He offers His grace. Let's be brave enough to tell the truth! Standing up to our enemy and taking back our homes and families from his clutches is pretty unexplainable. I'm praying for you, dear one. This *single step* of telling the truth may be the most unexplainable thing you ever do.

WEEK 4 | DAY 3
JEALOUS OF THE GOOD

Please read aloud ACTS 5:12–20

In the midst of Ananias's and Sapphira's sin, the disciples continue performing miraculous signs and wonders. We still see unity among the believers. They continue to maintain their Jewish heritage and customs as well.

Read Acts 5:12–16.

Where were the believers meeting?

This large area ran along the east side of the outer court of the temple. It afforded the apostles a covered area where large numbers of people could gather. It was called Solomon's portico because it was believed to have been a remnant of the original temple completed by King Solomon back in 959 BC.[11]

In light of the story of Ananias and Sapphira, why do you suppose some people did not dare join them?

In spite of the reluctance by some to join in their worship, what was happening nonetheless?

What did some people who were not yet believers do in order to receive healing?

Describe Peter's ability to heal the sick and demon-possessed.

As we see, many people came for healing. Many of these may have joined the group of believers, though others may not have. Have you ever witnessed someone come to Christ in search of an immediate fix for a problem, but then their resolve to follow Him didn't last? Describe that situation.

Why do you think their commitment fizzled?

Read Acts 5:17–20.
Who is mentioned in verse 17 and what was their reaction to the apostles' following? What did they do?

Who foiled their plan?

What instruction was given?

I love how the angel commands them to present the gospel. Your translation may say "the full message," "all the words," or "all about" this new life. In others words, don't water it down. Don't make the message less controversial due to fear of the temple authorities. Tell the whole truth—even the part that will be hard for hearers to receive.

Here's a good reminder for us—it's easy to tell people that Jesus loves them, but hard to talk to them about their sin. It's easy to share God's grace, but uncomfortable to warn of His judgment.

Do people alter the message of Jesus today? How?

Why do you suppose people are tempted to water down the gospel in hopes of making Jesus more appealing?

If you were to share the gospel with someone, write out below what you would say:

When and where did you first hear the gospel? What was the hardest part for you to understand/accept?

How does Paul describe the message of the gospel in 1 Corinthians 1:18–21?

What warning did Paul give in 2 Corinthians 11:4, 13–15?

Just because people won't believe the message does not mean we should be silent. Even if it is offensive, we still must tell. Even if it puts us in danger, we must speak. Courage and resolve in the face of danger or rejection is completely unexplainable.

> There is not a greater service done to the devil's kingdom than the silencing of faithful ministers, and putting those under a bushel that are the lights of the world.[12]

Who can you tell the full message of this new life?

Pray for His boldness and timing.

WEEK 4 | DAY 4
A GUILT TRIP!
Please read aloud ACTS 5:21–40

The first time I stepped foot in our Arizona state prison, terror consumed me. The gate rolled open allowing me to step into a holding area called a sally port. Once the gate rolled shut behind me, a solid steel door creaked open allowing me to enter the prison yard. As the steel door lagged closed behind me, I began to sweat uncontrollably. Countless what-ifs flooded my mind, and I felt that my heart would beat right out of my chest. What if I needed to get out of here? What if something dangerous erupted? I could die a thousand deaths before that steel door rolled open wide enough for me to escape! Standing out in a giant prison yard, I suddenly felt claustrophobic. I apologized profusely to the prison chaplain, embarrassed by how I was acting. He smiled. "Don't worry," he said, "everybody has a bit of a reaction the first time they're inside. You'll get used to it." He was right. Prison ministry became the highlight of my week, but I will never forget the first time that gate slammed shut behind me.

I thought about the apostles and their jail experience. Peter and John had already been through this once, but what were they all thinking and feeling? I wonder how many hours passed before the angel arrived.

What might you have been thinking and feeling if you were the apostles?

After the angel's appearance, do you think it was easier for the apostles to return to the temple and preach, or even more frightening? Why do you believe as you do?

See Acts 5:21–23.
At what time of day did the apostles return to the temple?

What did the high priest and the rest of the Sanhedrin do as soon as they arrived at the temple in the morning?

Just as the angel had somehow ushered the apostles past the prison guards the night before, chances are the members of the Sanhedrin had also walked right past the apostles teaching in the temple and not even seen them. I think this is quite telling. Obviously the apostles' teaching failed to create any sort of unrest within the temple. For all the Sanhedrin knew, the crowd gathered in the corner was any other group of Jewish men discussing the laws of Torah or contemplating prophecy. The gathering was orderly and respectful, not at all the discord the Sanhedrin tried to make it out to be!

Now read Acts 5:24–28.
Describe the reaction of the chief priests and temple guard.

What did they learn the former prisoners were now doing?

What insight does verse 26 give us about most people's feelings toward the apostles?

What was the chief concern of the high priest in this passage?

Once again, the Sanhedrin sat in a true catch-22. As the religious leaders of the day, how in the world could they ever confess that they had failed to recognize the promised Messiah, let alone concede that they had crucified him? On the other hand, the apostles' unexplainable courage, wisdom, and miraculous deeds could not be denied. What in the world were they to do? To acknowledge that the apostles' power came from God meant the acceptance of their message as truth. They just wanted it all to go away, but the apostles would not keep silent.

Read Acts 5:29–31.
For what reason did Peter insist he must continue to preach?

Did Peter try to alleviate the guilt of the Sanhedrin?

By what two titles did Peter call Jesus in Acts 5:31? (If you are using the ESV, look up these titles in an alternative translation. Biblegateway.com is a handy site for checking multiple versions.)

What two abilities did Peter ascribe to Jesus?

Let's go back to the book of Ezekiel, 34:23–26. What do verses 23–24 tell us about the prince?

What special relationship does the prince have with God according to Ezekiel 44:3?

Look carefully at Ezekiel 44:1–4 and Acts 5:12. Consider this description: "Solomon's porch was on the east side of the temple . . . the south portico was called Solomon's because people thought that its pre-Herodian masonry had survived from Solomon's temple."[13]

What do you learn about this location?

What else does Peter suggest Jesus gave to the apostles in Acts 5:32?

How does this also tie in with Ezekiel's prophecy in 36:26–27?

Peter speaks inflammatory words from Ezekiel's messianic prophecies to boldly proclaim that Jesus is the promised Messiah. In other words, Peter says, "You think I'm trying to make you guilty of unjustly murdering an innocent man? Oh yes, you'd better believe I am!"

See Acts 5:33–40. How did the Sanhedrin react to Peter's declaration?

Who calmed the Jewish high court, and what did he suggest?

What warning did he issue?

Have you ever gone through a situation in life where you now look back and see that you were "opposing God"? What did you learn from that experience?

What do you think Gamaliel thought of the apostles? Explain your answer.

Unlike Peter and John's release in Acts 4:21, what did the Sanhedrin do differently?

The heat has been turned up high. To preach the name of Jesus involves imprisonment and suffering. What will the apostles do? What would *you* do?

WEEK 4 | DAY 5
WORTHY OF SUFFERING
Please read aloud ACTS 5:41–42

The Voice of the Martyrs releases gripping and inspirational stories of our brothers and sisters around the world who suffer for their faith. These faithful servants are true heroes to me: Hebrews 11 kind of Christians. Their burden for the gospel to go forth and the glory of God to be revealed far outweighs what I witness within myself on most days. Inspired by their perseverance, I pray for an end to their suffering, along with the plea that in the wake of persecution, I might be counted as faithful as they are.

Describe the apostles' reaction to their flogging in Acts 5:41:

Luke's description of their reaction intrigued me.

What do you think it means to be "considered worthy" or "counted worthy" to suffer in Jesus' name?

Luke implies that suffering is an honor only bestowed on a select few of Jesus' followers. Not just anyone is up for the task. Is the person who is called to suffer somehow more spiritual or faithful? In the United States, we are beginning to see glimpses of persecution for our faith. (Paul Nyquist's *Prepare: Living Your Faith in an Increasingly Hostile Culture* cites sobering examples of our changing society and offers doable responses.) Physical beatings are probably still a long way off, but our American Christian response stands in marked contrast from this response of the early believers. We mobilize on social media in protest. We rant about our rights. We demand that the authorities acknowledge injustice. We threaten legal action. After all, it seems un-American to not stand for our rights.

So how do we, in this day and age, interpret this verse in Scripture? Are we to emulate the apostles' attitude, or interpret their response in light of their current governmental situation and rejoice that we live in a country with a first amendment to our constitution?

How do you think we, as American Christians, should apply this verse?

How far are you willing to go to defend your right to speak the name of Jesus publicly?

To be honest, I'm still wrestling with a solid answer as to a biblical course of action. There are a lot more gray areas than there are black and white ones. I do believe we need to resolve to stand for Jesus and acknowledge our faith in Him no matter what the consequences.

There is a fine line between defending the name of Jesus and defending our right to publicly proclaim it. However, the changing tide of our culture demands that we diligently seek the Lord for our proper course of action in specific situations. We are moving into an era where it is no longer a what-if, hypothetical scenario; it's a real question citizens of America are currently facing.

One thing we can learn from this passage of Scripture is that persecution ignited fire in the early believers' hearts rather than squelched it. Despite persecution, threats, and intimidation, they continued to boldly proclaim the name of Jesus.

Look carefully at Acts 5:42.
Where did the apostles meet?

When did they meet?

What did they do?

What was their message?

I hope you picked up on something new here, but in case you didn't, I'm going to explicitly point it out to you. Previously the apostles taught in the temple courts. Now they are teaching in the temple and going *house to house*. While the Sanhedrin schemed to minimize the message, the opposite resulted. The gospel went to the towns and villages. The apostles no longer parked themselves on Solomon's porch and waited for the Jewish people to come to them; they took the gospel out to the people—in their everyday lives going about their daily routines.

Christian persecution may or may not spread in America in our lifetime. But if it should, I hope the result is the same as it was for the apostles—the subsequent spread of the gospel!

What is a practical way you can take the gospel to people in their everyday lives and activities?

If you were to identify one primary reason why you don't regularly share your faith with others, what would it be?

Have you ever been in a situation in which you felt shame, disgrace, or humiliation for your faith? What has today's lesson taught you about God allowing you to go through that situation?

Whether you or I will ever be counted worthy of suffering for the name of Jesus, only the Name Above All Names knows. In the meantime, we need to make the gospel known as clearly and as often as we can. After all, if God is for us, who can be against us? Standing strong in the face of humiliation or persecution is about as unexplainable as it gets, isn't it?

unexplainable vision

FIRST THINGS FIRST

Please read aloud ACTS 6:1–7

Discussing Christian persecution is hardly a fun topic. However, we saw in Week 4 how God used the threats of the Sanhedrin to multiply the spread of the gospel into the city of Jerusalem and the surrounding villages. We are going to see something even more exciting today!

Read Acts 6:1 and record the first part of verse 1 below:

Does that excite anybody besides me? We know we have a real enemy. Despite real spiritual opposition to the gospel that we can sense and see in events played out around the world, the gospel will continue to go forth. God will continue to draw people's hearts to His. The Holy Spirit will call and convict. Of this we can be sure!

Of course, the greater the number of people, the greater the difficulties. This is a tried and true principle as well.

Read Acts 6:1–7.
What problem has arisen in the church?

What did the apostles insist their calling to be within the church, and what did they suggest be done about the issue?

What would this plan allow them to do?

How did all the believers respond to their idea?

Now that, my friend, is a church committee on which I'd love to serve! One hundred percent agreement! You *know* we're talking divine intervention when that's the case.

List the seven deacons:

What additional information does Luke give in regard to Nicolaus?

How did the apostles validate the choice of the seven?

What happened as a result of this division of labor within the church leadership according to Acts 6:7?

Approach any pastor in the western world and nearly all of them will give you the same statistic about their church family: twenty percent of the people are doing 80 percent of the work. And the pastor and his wife are probably picking up the slack for the remaining 20 percent. I hope today's story spurs you to consider how you might serve within your church. The apostles were working day and night preaching, praying, and overseeing the needs of this infant church. The number of needs grew so rapidly, they began to detract from their ability to teach and preach.

The widows' immediate needs demanded attention. They couldn't be ignored or put off until a more convenient time. But the mission of the apostles was the spread of the gospel. When the apostles were released to fulfill their primary mission, the gospel began to spread rapidly. Also when more people were called to step in and serve, we saw additional people come to faith as they witnessed the strong community of the church in action.

I can think of a couple of reasons people may not be serving in their local church. One is that sometimes we only want to serve in a place that makes us feel good. Another is that we wait to serve until something comes up that perfectly matches our skills and passion.

My friend Jennifer is a brilliant woman. She runs circles around me intellectually and her people skills are exceptional. You know what Jennifer does the first Sunday of every month? She makes coffee. Then she washes the coffee pots and puts them away. She does it to *serve her church family*. It's not high profile. She's more than capable of participating in dozens of other ministry assignments, but she makes the coffee and cleans up because she knows it needs to be done. Few coffee drinkers may have taken the time to thank Jennifer, but she still does it the first Sunday of every month. This is service.

A natural fit and personal passion toward a particular task or role are not necessarily required for your service to be effective. It doesn't take a lot of natural skills to vacuum carpets or empty trash cans. Just about anybody can fold a bulletin or take attendance. Most of us are already preparing meals for our own families and could easily make a little extra to take to a family in need. Sometimes service is just about getting work done, not about our egos, how we're wired, and where we thrive.

I believe a willingness to serve in any area where there is a hole to be filled says a lot about a person. It also equips us to recognize needs more readily. When we're repeatedly exposed to simple areas of need around us, our minds and hearts become more attuned to opportunities regularly presented throughout the week. Rather than always thinking about how service benefits us or makes us feel, we start to look outward.

Are you currently serving somewhere in your church?

If you aren't, can you think of ways to get involved?

What does Peter say about serving in the church in 1 Peter 4:10–11?

Look back at Acts 6:5; how is Stephen described?

With a description like that, you'd think he would be called to teach and preach. I'd love that description on my epitaph: *Here lies Erica, a woman full of faith and the Holy Spirit!* Do you get where I'm going with this? A man full of faith and the Holy Spirit was called to run a food bank. If you were one of the widows who depended on Stephen for your very sustenance, would you want him to be any other kind of man? To the people he was called to serve, he was indispensable.

Consider this adage that fits the theme of today's lesson perfectly:

> To the world you may only be one person,
> but to one person you may be the world.

Whose world can you impact today? Maybe it's as simple as making someone a cup of coffee, but if it's done with a servant's heart, it's unexplainable nonetheless.

WEEK 5 | DAY 2
RADIANT

Please read aloud ACTS 6:8–15

Luke's contrasting reports give us insight into the primary ways our enemy brings opposition against the church. Look at each incident below and match it with whom the enemy used as instruments:

PETER AND JOHN HEALING THE LAME MAN   OTHER BELIEVERS

ANANIAS AND SAPPHIRA   GOVERNMENTAL/CIVIL AUTHORITIES

THE WIDOWS' FOOD DISTRIBUTION

THE APOSTLES' MIRACULOUS HEALING
OF MANY PEOPLE

Now match the method he used to each situation:

PERSECUTION/INTIMIDATION   PETER AND JOHN HEALING THE LAME MAN

CORRUPTION/HYPOCRISY   ANANIAS AND SAPPHIRA

DISTRACTIONS   THE WIDOWS' FOOD DISTRIBUTION

      THE APOSTLES' MIRACULOUS HEALING
OF MANY PEOPLE

Luke raises awareness that our enemy works within the church as readily as he works outside of it. Both his instruments and his methods demonstrate this. We must pray diligently for the purity of our church and for protection over it, so the enemy is unable to make insidious inroads causing division and strife.

Luke continually guides us through the story at a good pace, but occasionally I wish I could grab him by the arm and say, "Luke, wait! Explain that a little more. What exactly is happening here?"

That, my friend, is how I feel with yesterday's and today's passage. He throws in all these people groups expecting us to understand what he means. I hope by the end of today we'll have slowed down long enough to take away some of his key points.

Read Stephen's description in Acts 6:8, then compare it with how he was described in Acts 6:5. How do you see faith and the Holy Spirit linking together with grace and power?

Who began to oppose Stephen, but what were they unable to do? See Acts 6:9–10.

Here is one place where I wish we could pull Luke aside and ask him to give us some more information. I thought Stephen was running a food bank. So who are these men and why is Stephen engaged in a debate with them? That is what we'll try to uncover today.

At this time in Jerusalem there were many separate synagogues outside the temple. These synagogues were primarily composed of small groups of Jews who had previously resided in other parts of the world, but had now returned to the holy city of Jerusalem. Their worship was conducted within their most comfortable language. The members were Jewish people by ethnicity, but they had lived for so long in a foreign country that their language adapted to the culture in which they had lived. The Synagogue of the Freedmen was most likely made up of Hellenistic Jews—or Jewish people who had been deeply influenced by the Greek and Roman culture. Their native language was Greek.

Different commentators speculate widely on the customs and religious culture of these Hellenistic Jews. Some assert that years of living in a culture opposed to Judaism resulted in strict adherence to Mosaic Law and fierce resolve in the maintenance of Jewish customs. Others propose that Greek liberality imposed on them at such length resulted in laxity and sophistry in their religious ordinances and observances. I don't think we can lump a large group of individuals into any one category. Living and worshiping alongside Christians as long as I have in several different subcultures of the United States and church denominations, I would suggest both camps of commentators are probably right.

Interestingly, these Hellenistic Jews are the same group who complained that their widows were being treated unfairly. If we look carefully at Acts 6:5, we discover that the seven deacons were all Hellenistic Jews themselves, minus Nicolaus, who wasn't Jewish at all! How do we conclude that? All seven of these men had Greek names rather than Hebrew ones. We also know that we cannot slap a carte blanche label of spiritual laxity on this sect of Jews, because these Jewish converts are described as men of noble character and strong faith.

Stephen's interaction with them possibly arose for a couple of different reasons. Since Stephen himself was a Hellenistic Jew, he may have been a member of this synagogue prior to his conversion. Also, the Hellenistic Jews often thought of themselves as intellectually superior to native Palestinian Jews, while the Palestinian Jews thought of themselves as more "purely Jewish" than their brothers who had been corrupted by pagan philosophies. If someone was going to debate with a Hellenistic Jew, it made sense for it to be another Greek-speaking, Hellenistic Jew like Stephen.

However, all of man's wisdom never can match the Holy Spirit, and Stephen ran circles around them in their debates. In their frustration, they took the debate to a whole new level.

Read Acts 6:11–14.

What did the men from this synagogue do?

What do you think these men did to "stir up" the people?

What charges did they bring against Stephen? Circle all that apply.

blasphemy

desecration of the temple

disrespect of the law of Moses

rebellion against the Roman government

negation of the promised Holy Land of Israel

teaching the doctrine of bodily resurrection

This scene plays out very differently than when the apostles had faced the Sanhedrin earlier. In that scenario, the Sanhedrin feared treating the apostles forcefully because of how highly regarded they were by the people. In Stephen's story, the Synagogue of the Freedmen successfully incited the people against him. Part of their ability to create such a stir among the Sanhedrin may have been because Stephen was not a Palestinian Jew himself, while the members of the Sanhedrin were. The Freedman capitalized on the cultural bias the Palestinian Jews held against them.

Additionally, Stephen's identity was probably not widely known outside the confines of the church. Unlike Peter or John, who were notable figures in Jerusalem at this time, Stephen was another Jewish man on the corner. He had not won the people's admiration for miraculous works as Peter and John had. The crowd hurls accusations about Stephen in front of the Sanhedrin. Frenzied onlookers demand the religious leaders to take action.

In the midst of the chaos, describe Stephen, according to Acts 6:15.

Here sat Stephen with the face of an angel. Calm and serene. Focused on another realm. Peacefully removed from the strife and chaos swirling around him. Pretty unexplainable apart from God. No wonder the Sanhedrin could not turn their gaze from him to meet the eyes of his accusers. They were too in awe of his response to them. Luke implies that Stephen's face is radiant, just as Moses's face had been when he returned from receiving the Law on top of Mt. Sinai. The accusers insist Stephen disregards Moses's law, yet here he sits resembling him in both appearance and demeanor!

I imagine a judge and jury often studies the face of the accused, reading their body language and facial expressions. A shift in their seat, a dart of the eye, or movement of the hands can quickly reveal inward emotional reactions to spoken words. Professionals even vocationally study mannerisms to determine if people are lying or telling the truth! Here sat Stephen completely disengaged from the angry mob, in the world, but not of it.

Stephen will become engaged when the time is right, but for now he remains unexplainably at peace in the face of his accusers.

HISTORY IS HIS STORY

Please read aloud ACTS 7:1–54

We have witnessed Luke's writing style to be "Only the facts, just the facts, please!" He writes in simple, straightforward sentences. Yet in Stephen's sermon Luke methodically records every single word, highlighting the significance of its contents.

I pored more deeply through this section of Acts than any other chapter. The connections Stephen was making and the subsequent applications seemed endless. We see Stephen's Greek influence shine center stage in his masterful retelling of the history of Israel. He expertly highlights segments of Israel's history to not only refute the accusations brought against him, but to form an argument of his own: *What you are doing to me right at this moment is exactly what our forefathers have done throughout our history to every prophet who stood before them.*

Read Acts 7:1–5.
What does the high priest ask Stephen?

How does Stephen address the Sanhedrin?

By what name does Stephen refer to God?

With whom does Stephen begin the history of Israel?

Where did Abraham go first, and when did he finally arrive in Canaan?

Was Abraham given the land or was he given a promise? See verse 5.

Through this passage, Stephen refutes his first accusation and makes his first argument. In essence he says, "Listen, I'm going to spell this all out for you. While I do, my prayer is that God will speak to you through it and you will finally hear His voice. He will reveal to you that Jesus is indeed the promise that was to come!" Then he refutes their accusation that he has spoken against the Promised Land of Israel by asserting that he agrees wholeheartedly that the land is theirs through an irrefutable promise of God.

Read Acts 7:6–17.
What did God say would happen prior to Abraham's descendants inhabiting the land?

What covenant did God give Abraham?

What word does Stephen use to describe the brothers' feelings toward Joseph?

How did the people of Israel end up in Egypt?

Where were Jacob's descendants buried?

What promise did God fulfill to Abraham?

Stephen expertly slides in a second argument that tacks on to his first one: *God's fulfillment of promises did not depend on the location of His people.* In other words, the promises were fulfilled by and through God's power. In the minds of the Israelites, the promises were tied to the land. So if Israel did not possess Canaan, God's promises were unable to be fulfilled. Without the temple, God would be unable to dwell among them. Stephen points out that God's promises to Abraham were fulfilled despite the fact that he never possessed the land of Canaan. Next, Stephen tackles the accusation of speaking blasphemy against Moses and God's law given through him.

Read Acts 7:23–37.
What happened when Moses was forty years old? How did the Israelites respond? See verses 23–27.

Where did Moses go and why?

What happened forty years later?

How does Stephen describe Moses in verse 35?

What else does he say about Moses in the rest of the passage we read?

Stephen confirms Moses's selection by God as the chosen leader and deliverer of Israel from Egyptian bondage. He also insists that the Mosaic Law was given to him directly by God Himself. Stephen refers to the Mosaic Law as "living oracles" (v. 38), intimating that God continues to speak through this law. Furthermore, he reminds them of Moses's promise that God would send them a prophet like him.

Stephen also parallels Moses with Joseph. Both men were chosen by God to rule over their Israelite brothers and both of them were rejected the first time their authority was revealed. The second time God raised them up to rule, however, their brothers acquiesced. This, of course, is Stephen's current hope for his audience when it comes to their submission to Jesus as the Christ.

> For teaching on Amos 5, which Stephen quotes in his sermon, check out Deeper Discoveries at ericawiggenhorn.com.

Read Acts 7:44–50.
What does Stephen say about the tabernacle (tent of witness)?

Who eventually built the temple, the "dwelling place" for God?

What does Stephen say about the temple in verses 48–50?

He moves into his third refutation regarding the desecration of the temple. He outlines the construction of the temple as ordained and instructed by God. The argument he throws in, however, is that despite the existence of the tabernacle and temple, idolatry remained throughout Israel. While the Jewish people believed that the temple site bridged heaven to earth, the existence of the temple failed to purify Israel. He further emphasizes that proper worship was not dependent on the establishment of these structures.

Stephen's arguments are quite inflammatory, but he doesn't stop here.

What does Stephen say to the Sanhedrin in Acts 7:51–53?

I wonder, did his face look angelic now? Stephen's sermon selectively parallels their responses to Joseph, Moses, and God to their response to Jesus. The Jewish people believed that their national identity and proper worship within the temple prompted God to keep His promises. In other words, man's actions determined God's steps.

Herein lies Stephen's overarching point: Just like our forefathers missed Joseph and Moses, you have missed the Messiah. You have resisted the clarity of Jesus Christ's identity, but the truth of it will spread throughout Israel regardless. The coming of the Messiah was never dependent upon what we do or don't do, but entirely based on the irrefutable promises and power of God. The kingdom is Christ, the temple is Christ, fulfilled through us: God's chosen people.

And let's face it, friend. When God's involved, it's always unexplainable.

WEEK 5 | DAY 4
LOOKING UP
Please read aloud ACTS 7:48–60

I wish Luke told us what Stephen's face resembled beginning with Acts 7:51! Personally I think Stephen's voice got louder and his pace quickened. I have no doubt some members of the Sanhedrin knew where his speech was headed as soon as he got to verse 42. I highly doubt any of them expected him to become so accusatory, though. The tension in the air must have been thick enough to slice.

Read Acts 7:54–56.
How did the Sanhedrin respond to Stephen's accusations?

In contrast, describe Stephen in this passage.

Amidst the shouts of the members of the Sanhedrin demanding Stephen's swift execution, Stephen again speaks. In desperation he motions, shouting for the crowd to look, but his pleas were drowned out in the waves of the crowd's powerful fury.

Angry, bloodthirsty men are shouting so loudly it is uncertain how many of them were even able to hear Stephen. Much like Jesus' trial before Pontius Pilate, the crowd wanted blood. Chanting, grinding their teeth, pounding their fists, stamping their feet, they demanded immediate action by the high priest. "Blasphemy! Blasphemy! This man deserves death! Kill him! *Kill him!* KILL HIM!!!" Their frenzy would not be calmed until he was punished. The chanting grew louder and faster, waiting for the nod of the high priest's head for permission to drag Stephen outside the city to stone him. Barely perceptible amidst the furious men, the slight lowering of the chin of the high priest, the vengeful crowd rushed upon Stephen, pummeling him while pushing him toward the exit to the courtroom. They could not get him outside the city fast enough. Who knows who relayed Stephen's vision to the early believers so Luke was able to record what Stephen saw with such clarity? Maybe Saul, who is first introduced to us in this violent scene, recounted the event to Luke in later years.

In light of Stephen's vision, recall what Jesus told the Sanhedrin in Luke 22:66–71.

What do we learn about how we are ushered into heaven in Jude 24? Write that beautiful verse here and savor this promise!

I can imagine Jesus standing as Stephen's witness, testifying to his righteousness before His Father. Stephen was Christ's first martyr. The word martyr actually means witness, but with such intense persecution of early Christians, the word became synonymous with someone who would witness their belief in Christ even to death. I also imagine Jesus preparing to present Stephen to His Father and to welcome him with great joy! When reading accounts like these, does it make them more personal to picture them in your mind's eye?

This story of Stephen's martyrdom is often read quickly while studying the book of Acts. We don't especially want to dwell on his story because it is so painful, but I believe it is one of the most profound scenes in Scripture. It's a life-changing passage we shouldn't miss. I have taken some creative license here to help us imagine what it might have been like for Stephen.

While Jesus stood in front of His throne gazing at His beloved child, the frenetic shouts of the crowd escalated. "Blasphemy!" they cried. "Kill him! Silence him quickly!" They covered their ears with their hands as rebellious children refusing to listen to their wise parent. "No more! Silence! We cannot hear any more of your lies!"

Stephen insisted, "Look! Look up!" but to no avail. Like a swarm of bloodthirsty, wild beasts they surrounded Stephen, ushering him out of the building by the weight of their force. He fell under the pressure of the mob. Stomping on his chest and kicking his head they reached for his limbs to drag him outside the city. All he could see was the hatred in their eyes and the spit on their lips as it flew upon his cheeks and forehead. Unable to discern their words amidst the furious shouts, he prayed. Again, he caught a glimpse of his beloved Savior, standing in His honor. Stephen tried to get the mob to turn heavenward, but they were too busy clearing a path through the city.

The gravel ripped his back and thighs as they dragged him through the streets. The shouting around him was deafening. Eventually they arrived to an acceptable place to inflict the slow and painful death of stoning. Throwing him to the ground the mob began hurling any sized rock they could find. Faster and faster the stones attacked his flesh. He grew dizzy and his heartbeat slowed. He knew death was near. Still looking up he prayed to Jesus yet again. Praying his accusers would see the glory of God, he continued to keep his eyes on his King. But their backs were bent in rebellion, continuing to search for more stones to cast.

Falling to his knees he cried out with the last burst of energy he could muster, "Lord, do not hold this sin against them!" Can you imagine such forgiveness in the midst of such pain? Stephen then gave up his spirit. The hurling rocks slowed; finally, the last few men holding stones dropped them to the ground, unneeded. Punishment according to the law had been inflicted. Zeal for the Mosaic Law upheld. Yet the Sanhedrin felt no peace.

If only they had looked up. Think of what they missed. It would have been the day of salvation for this angry mob. If only they had seen the glory of God. Instead they looked inwardly at their own self-righteousness and indignation at Stephen's suggestion they might have missed something. Where is your gaze resting today, friend? Are you looking at the crowd? Your circumstances? Or are you looking to Jesus?

Let's pause and take a few moments to remember our brothers and sisters in Christ across the globe who are suffering unspeakable persecution. Write a prayer here for them.

Notice what Paul wrote later in Philippians 1:28. Do you think he recalled Stephen's countenance on this day when he penned that letter?

When we remember that we have a Witness in heaven, one who declares us righteous and His, one who is seated on the edge of His throne waiting to welcome us home, all the while praying intently over us until the moment of our arrival, our perspective changes (Hebrews 7:25). Does it really matter what anybody else thinks of us? Will our circumstances affect where we spend eternity? Look up, friend. Jesus is for you. He is working out every detail of your life for His glory and your good. And it's going to be unexplainable.

SAUL DOES NOT SEE

Please read aloud ACTS 7:58–8:1

Prior to the martyrdom of Stephen, the Sadducees brought charges against the apostles. This aristocratic group denounced miracles, the existence of angels, and bodily resurrection. Since all three of these were fundamental components of the gospel story, coupled with continual miraculous signs performed by the apostles, they logically attacked the early church.

The Pharisees, however, were legalists and interpreted the miracles recorded in the Old Testament in a literal fashion. They believed in miracles, bodily resurrection, and the existence of angelic beings. In fact, it was the Pharisees who taught that Jewish corpses could not be resurrected outside the city of Jerusalem. Any Jewish corpse would have to make its way back into the city via the underworld. Their legalism and strong traditions incited their anger toward Stephen due to his suggestion that the true temple was Christ Jesus.

Once the Pharisees began to oppose the early church, great persecution broke out. Their zeal for Christian persecution paralleled their zeal for strict adherence to the Mosaic Law and protection of their traditions. Luke introduces us to one Pharisee in particular.

What was Saul's role in Stephen's stoning, according to Acts 7:58?

The mob's level of anger rose exponentially. They took off their outer garments, enabling them to hurl stones at Stephen with even greater force. They sought to brutally pummel him. Ancient literature reveals the removal of the outer cloak prior to an act of violence, usually resulted in murder.[14] No mercy here whatsoever. In an angry frenzy this mob of men ripped off their coats to gather stones.

They laid their garments at the feet of a young man named Saul. This seemingly small detail alerts us to the fact that Saul most likely served as the ringleader of this angry mob.[15] Leading the men from the synagogue to the court, he quite possibly first presented the case to the Sanhedrin, riling up the crowd as he dramatically argued for a charge of blasphemy against Stephen. As guardian of the coats, he stood as the one in authority over the execution. I believe this moment in Saul's life impacted him greatly, because he refers back to it often in his writings. He undoubtedly replayed this day in his mind over and over throughout his life.

What else does Luke tell us in Acts 7:60?

But oh, the mercy of our God! In a very short while, Saul would discover that at this moment—while he zealously instigated, stood in authority over the scene, nodded and approved—this angry mob murdered an innocent man. And not just an innocent man, but a righteous witness for the promised Savior and Messiah. We know how greatly Saul, who became the apostle Paul, agonized over his persecution of the church before his conversion. In this scene, Saul had used his incredible teaching skills to convince a crowd of people to murder someone. God, in His very great mercy, would redeem Saul's skills to convince countless thousands of the truth of Christ under the guidance of the Holy Spirit. Saul would spend the rest of his life in awe of this mercy of God as he zealously preached Christ with even greater fervor than he had persecuted Him. That mercy, my friend, is utterly unexplainable.

What does Paul say about himself in 1 Corinthians 15:9?

What else does Paul say about himself in 1 Timothy 1:15–16? Read these verses out loud.

What does Paul say in 2 Corinthians 4:1 we must not do now that we have been shown mercy?

When we are consumed with guilt and shame it's pretty easy to lose heart or give up, isn't it? However, what evil intended to use to incapacitate us, God takes and uses to drive us even harder in our service to Him.

What did the grace of God do for Paul in 1 Corinthians 15:10?

Our God is so faithful to take what has been used against us and turn it into good. This has always been His way.

What did Job say in Job 23:10?

What did Joseph say about all that he had endured in Genesis 50:20?

How do you suppose God could use difficult or rebellious circumstances in your past to bring about good?

Surely the apostles and early believers clung to God's ancient truth while grieving Stephen's death. But what good could possibly come from this? Luke immediately moves on to this point.

What happened in Acts 8:1?

Think about it. Up to this point the believers are gathering together daily, united in heart, prayer, and vision. God continuously performs incredible miracles in their midst. They are being taught by the mighty apostles while residing in their beloved holy city, Jerusalem. So until this point, the gospel primarily remained within the city's walls. Now obviously some of the migratory Jews who received the message on Pentecost returned to their surrounding villages and outlying cities at the conclusion of the feast.

Jesus had commanded them to carry the gospel to the rest of Israel, however, and in the right time, it would happen. In the midst of great grief and sudden persecution, the gospel spreads. God took evil and used it for good. Just as He always has done. When communism first infiltrated China in 1949, the church only grew under its persecution, rather than be wiped out as the atheistic government planned. Could it be that Jesus longs to take the tragedy, injustice, hurt, betrayal, rebellion, or past sin in your life and do something unexplainable with it? Do you suppose that He wants to bring you forth as gold for the saving of many people?

While Saul stood holding robes during Stephen's stoning he could not see it. Maybe you can't yet, either. Look up, friend. Ask for eyes to see. At this point in Acts the story of Saul has only just begun, and one thing I can promise you is that your story isn't finished yet either. The only question is: Will you insist on a predictable storyline for your life? Or will you allow Him to make your life unexplainable? Hand Him your past today. Remember what Job 23:10 said? Can you take this truth to heart?

AN UNEXPLAINABLE LIFE

unexplainable expansion

WEEK 6 | DAY 1
UNEXPLAINABLE EXPANSION
Please read aloud ACTS 8:1–5

Last week we examined God's remarkable way of taking evil and bringing something good from it. That theme becomes further developed today. The conflict among the early church and Jewish authorities came to a head, forcing many believers to flee outside Jerusalem's city walls. Some stayed, however, which can be concluded by studying the following verses.

Read Acts 8:1–5.
After Stephen's death, what did some of the believers do?

What did Saul do?

What did those who were scattered do?

Where did Phillip go?

The Sanhedrin expected to end the spread of the gospel once and for all through Stephen's martyrdom. Saul sought to cement the end of this movement by arresting believers and subjecting many of them to the same trial Stephen endured. Apparently after the Sanhedrin heard Stephen's sermon, they passed decrees making following Jesus a punishable crime (see Acts 22:4–5). Prior to this moment, the Sadducees and Pharisees, who historically disagreed with one another, failed to reach a consensus regarding what to do with the growing number of believers. After Stephen's trial, they united against their common enemy: the Jesus followers. Luke doesn't specify exactly what allowed Saul to haul them off to prison, whether active preaching in the temple courts or merely identification with the movement, but the rulers of the temple have clearly issued authority to have them imprisoned.

Look back at Acts 1:8 and record Jesus' last words to His apostles:

And so we see this exact story unfolding. Where specifically did the believers scatter, according to Acts 8:1?

These early believers still remained within the confines of the Promised Land of Israel. Although it had been the apostles whom Christ commissioned to spread the gospel message throughout Israel, the believers at large are those who actually carry it out. At this point it is widely thought the apostles still remained within the confines of Israel (see Acts 8:1 and 15:1–4). We see later in Peter's astonishment over Cornelius's conversion that the apostles still did not fully grasp God's intention to include the Gentiles in His kingdom, at least not in the way we understand it. They thought all Gentiles must convert to Judaism, and then as proselytes they would become eligible to follow the Messiah. While it did occur to them that they could preach the good news to these Gentile converts to Judaism, they still did not realize that Jesus meant sharing the good news with Gentiles who did not follow the law of Moses or worship Yahweh.

Jesus had stated that the apostles were to become His witnesses to the ends of the earth, but so far they had stood as witnesses only to their Jewish brethren. This should be a sobering reminder for us. The apostles continued to wrestle with full understanding of God's plans, and it required miraculous intervention for God to unveil their eyes. It's also encouraging for us. Despite our frailty and limitations in grasping the greatness of our God and the intricacy of His plans, He continues to call us. Over time the Holy Spirit continues to open our eyes, conform our hearts, and reveal Himself in more profound ways, allowing us greater understanding. Eventually through the work of Paul and others, all Gentiles would begin to hear the gospel message.

Have you ever felt God call you to do something, yet been unable to follow through in pursuing that call? What was it you felt called to do?

What prevented, or is currently preventing, you from pursuing it?

Have you sensed God allowing your circumstances to become increasingly uncomfortable in the midst of your unwillingness to proceed with His directives?

Did God force you to move in order for you to move forward in obedience?

What do you suppose made it so difficult for the apostles to comprehend God's inclusion of the Gentiles into His kingdom?

Jesus was not dependent on His original twelve apostles to complete His mission, any more than He is dependent on us to finish what He has started. His work *will be completed* regardless of your obedience or mine. However, He *invites* us to be a part of it and *faithfully equips* us to carry it out. He is exceedingly patient with us to follow His plans.

We can be too busy. We can stubbornly refuse in our fear. Jesus requires whole-hearted obedience. We must ask what He wants us to do, otherwise He may assign the work He intended for us to someone else. My biggest fear is standing before Him one day and being shown all the plans I missed. I want to do the work He sent me here on earth to do. I don't want to be robbed of one single step I can walk with Christ while on earth.

Let's stop right here for a moment and sit at the feet of Jesus. Ask the Holy Spirit to bring to mind anything God may have laid on your heart at one time but that you have forgotten about.

Ask Him to reveal to you any area of your life you have not fully surrendered to Him in obedience.

Ask Him to search your heart and reveal to you anything you need to confess.

Ask Him to show you where you have gotten comfortable and to reveal to you what a greater level of faith and obedience might look like in your life.

Record anything the Spirit reveals to you in the margin of your book, a journal, or in Acts 8 in your Bible, and today's date.

While the apostles were in Jerusalem, Philip, one of the seven who had been chosen along with Stephen to serve as a deacon, went to a unique place in Israel. We're told in verse 5 that he went to Samaria. I can assure you that if anyone had approached the apostles asking them to go and preach in the region of Samaria, their response would have been, "No, thank you!" No one wanted to go to Samaria. In fact, Jews would travel out of their way to avoid this region of Israel.

The Samaritans and Israelites held a long and bitter rivalry. Israel split into northern and southern kingdoms after Solomon's death. The northern kingdom was called Israel with Samaria as the capital, while the southern kingdom was called Judah with Jerusalem serving as its capital city. The northern kingdom set up their own system of worship under King Jeroboam, because he didn't want his citizens traveling to Jerusalem in the southern kingdom to worship in the temple. This was in direct opposition to God's law, and rampant idolatry resulted. Two hundred years later, the northern kingdom was conquered by the Assyrians and the Jews of the northern tribe intermarried with them. The Samaritans were the descendants of these mixed marriages.

Ironically, after the southern tribe had been exiled to Babylon and then returned to Israel to rebuild the temple, the northern Samaritans offered to help them. The southern Israelites spurned their offer, resulting in Samaritan conflict during the temple's construction under Nehemiah. The Samaritans then constructed their own temple on Mt. Gerazim, thereby separating their worship of Yahweh from their Jewish brethren in Jerusalem. Understanding this history sheds insight into the Samaritan woman's questions to Jesus in John 4.

Deeper Discoveries on the culture and people of Samaria can be found at ericawiggenhorn.com.

For Philip to go preach the gospel in Samaria says volumes about his character. Those who serve in ministries that reach out to gang members, the incarcerated community, and the homeless with the gospel are the "Philips" of today. The

Samaritans were social outcasts. Who in their right mind would waste their time trying to reach them?

Philip, that's who. Could it be that you have not pursued what God laid on your heart because it doesn't make a lick of sense to anybody around you? Is the mission you have been given so contrary to what's comfortable, socially acceptable, or even remotely possible when examined through the lens of common sense that you abandoned the idea before it went from a thought in your head to a prick in your heart?

Jesus' work is unexplainably unstoppable. We can either choose to be a part of it or remain comfortable. But as we'll see in tomorrow's story, we'd miss out on some amazing things!

PHILIP GOES TO SAMARIA

Please read aloud ACTS 8:6–8

My friend Debbie is a modern-day Philip. She felt called by God to start the ministry Beyond Fear to Freedom, whose primary aim is to bring to broken women the gospel of Jesus Christ. Realizing that these women feel uncomfortable in church, she started this ministry to offer another avenue to reach them. Homeless women, those in recovery, addicts, the abused, the downcast and downhearted—all are welcome to come and hear about the freedom Christ offers. The remarkable thing about Debbie's ministry is that the women who lead discipleship groups within it are former societal outcasts themselves, set free by their Savior Jesus Christ, and now leading other women to find that same freedom. It is beautiful to witness.

The most incredible part is their joy. They are so undone by the love of Jesus that they can't stop smiling. The passion their worship exudes puts me to shame. In the midst of all of their love and excitement for Jesus, they witness Him do loving and exciting things—victory over addictions, restoration within families, freedom from fear and self-destruction, and a renewed purpose for living.

Philip's trip to Samaria did the same thing in the lives of those to whom he preached.

Describe the Samaritans' reaction to Philip in Acts 8:6.

We now have record of another non-apostle performing miraculous signs. The first was Stephen. Philip has been given the ability as well.

Read Acts 8:7–8.

Describe the miracles that Philip performed and the people's reaction.

This is the first time Luke records either the apostles or anyone else *casting out* evil spirits after Jesus' ascension (though Matthew's and Mark's gospels refer to the disciples doing so). Previously he mentions the apostles healing those who were *tormented* by evil spirits, but in this passage he highlights Philip's work. I don't think Luke is using a different expression to make himself sound like a more gifted writer; I think the difference is spiritually significant. Philip has been granted a power over the spiritual realm that had yet to be experienced independently by the apostles since Jesus' departure. In Acts 5:16, Luke uses *ochleo* to describe the people's condition. This word could be translated "mobbed or harassed."[16] In Acts 8:8 though, he describes the spirits being violently forced out of individuals, leaving them—the difference between "violently forced out" and "tormented" is significant.

Record what happened in Mark 9:17–29.

What did Jesus say was necessary to drive out the demon?

Why did Jesus perform so few miracles in Nazareth according to Matthew 13:53–58?

Describe what happened in Luke 10:17–20. What warning did Jesus give?

Let's put this all together. First, we know Philip was a man of deep humility, because he chose to take the gospel to the despised and rejected. Certainly God laid this mission on his heart through prayer and the Holy Spirit. Second, unlike the Palestinian Jews who received the gospel hesitantly or skeptically, the Samaritans listened intently with eagerness and joy. As a result of their great faith in Jesus Christ, the Holy Spirit upped the ante. He began to drive out demons. Philip's willingness to be obedient to God in taking the gospel to Samaria made him a trustworthy candidate for God to begin to do even greater works.

What do you suppose the Lord knew about Philip that He chose to send him to Samaria?

We cannot put the ways of God into a convenient box or predict how the Holy Spirit will work. One thing that is incredibly consistent though, is that He chooses to move through faith-filled, obedient saints who are intent on glorifying God over accomplishing their own agenda. Philip obeyed God when it made absolutely no sense, involved great risk, and held little promise of reward. As a result, he witnessed the Spirit do a new thing.

What did Jesus tell Peter in Matthew 16:13–20?

This conversation occurred in Caesarea Philippi, a center of pagan worship. A river came out of a deep cave called the "Gates of Hades" at the bottom of a high rock cliff within this town. It was thought to be where the god Pan would return each year to bring fertility to the land.

> To learn more about the cultural significance of the cities Jesus visited with His disciples check out Deeper Discoveries at ericawiggenhorn.com.

God still has things He wants to show us of Himself. He has revealed truth in His Word, but we have yet to fully understand it all. Philip was willing to step into a life of greater obedience and as a result, he was the first to see Jesus' promises at Caesarea Philippi tangibly fulfilled. We must ever be careful that we are not building our own kingdoms for the sake of the kingdom. God called Philip to an unpopular place. Because of his faith and humility, he readily obeyed. And he witnessed even greater works.

Don't ignore those nudges, friend. Don't expect everyone else to understand the vision that God has entrusted to you. It is imperative to seek godly counsel. Search the Scripture intently for direction, be prayerful, and remain open. If it truly is His will, He will be faithful to confirm it through more than one source. It may not be everyone who understands your vision, but God will send someone if He is prompting you to act.

What did God tell His people in Isaiah 43:18–19?

God is able to do a new thing! Something never done before! Something unexplainable! He is looking for one person who is willing to go with Him to new places. Will you allow God to give you His vision for your life? He may send you somewhere you never thought you'd go. He may ask you to serve people with whom you have never interacted previously. One life of obedience multiplied a hundredfold—now that is some math that is pretty unexplainable!

Is there a particular people group, subculture, or population to which you feel drawn? An age group, such as children or the elderly, an ethnic group, socioeconomic class, or a marginalized segment of society? What could you do to serve these people in practical ways to open doors to share the gospel?

My friend Steve serves as a church consultant. He suggests that one of the most effective ways to share the gospel with our suburban friends and neighbors is to invite them to aid us in a cause. While your neighbors may not want to go with you to church on a Sunday morning, they may be much more willing to go with you to stock a food pantry or serve meals to the homeless. Our human souls have been created to be a part of something bigger than ourselves. Of course as believers we understand this search comes from our need for our Creator God. Your family's willingness to give up a Friday night to go serve strangers in need not only taps into your neighbor's searching soul, but also effectively opens the door for you to explain why you serve as you do—because of Christ. They need to see our faith not merely as a belief system, but put into action—even in, and especially in, places and ways that are unexplainable apart from God.

When the Lord looks on your heart, what do you suppose He sees—a person willing to follow Him anywhere?

Close today with a time of prayer. Confess to the Lord any fears you may have. If you are ready, echo some more words of Isaiah in your prayer: "Here I am, Lord! Send me!" (Isaiah 6:8)

THE PURPOSE OF THE POWER

Please read aloud ACTS 8:9–25

We have a lot to cover today, so I'm going to jump right into our passage. Read Acts 8:9–17.

Who was Simon, and what was his claim to fame?

What happened after Philip arrived in Samaria?

How did Simon respond? See verse 13.

The ability to perform miraculous signs and wonders does not guarantee that a person's power comes from God. In fact, Jesus warns us that many deceivers will come who are seemingly able to perform miracles. Scripture gives us some insight into how to discern the source of their power. First, when the apostles or deacons performed a miracle, they never accepted any sort of payment. When someone on television tells you to dial an 800 number while keeping your credit card handy so your miraculous healing can occur, that should be your first red flag! Second, the apostles and deacons never took credit for the miracle. They expressly emphasized that the power of Jesus performed the miracle—they held no ability within themselves. Finally, the miracles of the apostles and deacons resulted in great joy. Counterfeit miracles often result in awe and wonder, like Simon's miracles did in Acts 8:11, but the work of the Holy Spirit results in joy!

Luke intimates that Simon's "miracles" were mostly illusory in nature; however, after receiving Christ, the Samaritans repented from their affinity for Simon's occult practices. They were baptized and received the message with great joy.

Who came to witness the revival of Samaria?

According to verses 15–16, what had the Samaritan believers not yet received under Philip's ministry?

What happened in verse 17?

The reason why the Holy Spirit had not been made manifest in the lives of the Samaritan believers is sharply debated. I believe this order of events is best understood within the context of the longstanding history between the Samaritans and their Israelite brothers. As we discussed in Day 1 of this week, northern Samaria had set up its own system of worship after the split of Israel.

See John 4:19–24. What did the Samaritan woman say to Jesus and how did He respond?

Jesus is prophesying the unification of Samaria and Israel in their worship of God (recall Week 6 Day 1 and their separate temples on Mt. Gerazim and in Jerusalem.) The Jewish apostles traveling to Samaria for the Holy Spirit to become poured out over the Samaritans nullified the separation in systems of worship. The same apostles who delivered the gospel and Spirit at Pentecost would deliver it to the Samaritans. This was especially important since Philip was not one of the original twelve apostles. The Samaritans could have concluded their movement to be separate from what was happening within the walls of Jerusalem.

Further, due to the longstanding bias toward Samaritans by the Jews, the apostles themselves needed to publicly accept these despised people into the church. Maybe Peter and John would not have believed their repentance until they saw it with their own eyes! Maybe they needed to witness the miracles happening among the people of Samaria so God could begin to open their hearts for the spread of the gospel to the Gentiles.

As we will see in this next portion of Scripture, Peter's spiritual gift of discernment was needed in Samaria. While Philip was a tremendous evangelist and given the ability to work miracles, it takes every member of the body exercising their gifts together for the complete work of the kingdom to be accomplished.

See Acts 8:18–22. What is Simon's request?

What is Peter's response?

Look back at Acts 8:13 and read it carefully. Compare this with Peter's response to Simon in Acts 8:20–22. How do you reconcile the seeming contradiction?

Simon invited Christ's power into his life to use as he willed. He believed in Christ's power but he didn't want to surrender his life to being controlled by it. This is not what being a follower of Christ is about. Inviting Christ's power into our lives in order to accomplish *our* goals misunderstands the purpose of the power. The Holy Spirit's power is given to accomplish God's purposes, not our own. Until we surrender ourselves to Him, though our plans and goals may be good or noble, they may still conflict with what God longs to do. When we follow Christ in hopes that He will aid us in our own self-exaltation, whether that means monetary prosperity, transformational living for our own enjoyment, or achievement of personal goals that have never been given over to God, we have missed the entire point of the power of the gospel.

I love how Philippians 3:10 is rendered in the Amplified[17] version:

> [For my determined purpose is] that I may know Him [that I may progressively become more deeply and intimately acquainted with Him, perceiving and recognizing and understanding the wonders of His Person more strongly and more clearly], and that I *may in that same way come to know the power outflowing from His resurrection [which it exerts over believers]* (emphasis mine).

Simon had no concept of the person or work of the Holy Spirit. Why *does* God graciously give His Holy Spirit to His children? What is the Spirit's purpose? Let's examine the following passages:

John 14:26

Romans 8:27

1 Corinthians 2:9–10

1 Corinthians 12:7

How did Peter assess Simon's heart in Acts 8:23?

Simon's desire was not to be led into all truth, to sacrificially intercede for others, to build up others, nor to seek the common good. His search for the Spirit's power was to exalt himself. Why might we seek the power of the Holy Spirit in our lives?

Reflect on the following possibilities and jot down ideas that come to you.

For a tangible experience of God's blessing?

For victory over sin so our lives are easier or better?

To be revered as one of God's trophies who shares a powerful testimony in order to gain large audiences?

A sincere wish for Christ to be exalted?

Let's go back to Paul's words in Philippians 3:10 again and look at the rest of that verse in the Amplified version again:

> and that I may *so share His sufferings as to be continually transformed* [in spirit into His likeness even] to His death (emphasis mine).

How did Simon respond to Peter's assessment of his heart in Acts 8:24?

We are never too far away to receive God's grace when our hearts return to Him in repentance! Sin is deceptive. We can easily fall prey to its deceit and pray for personal gain. Our motives become blurred. Our ambitions quietly creep into hidden caverns of our heart. Fortunately, we have the Holy Spirit who searches all things—even these hidden spaces! Simon believed in Christ but he missed the point. After this account, we never hear of him again in the pages of Scripture.

You, my friend, have been given the Holy Spirit when you received the gospel and accepted Christ as your Savior. Just like Simon you may have seen His transforming power in others' lives but have yet to see it in your own. Maybe, like Simon, you have been asking the Spirit for the wrong thing. Maybe the work you have sought from Him has been about you rather than about Christ. Maybe you've never asked Him to work at all. He is within you, waiting to be brought forth.

Pray and ask what He longs to do in and through your life. Spend some time listening and record His answer below:

WEEK 6 | DAY 4
AS FAR AS AFRICA
Please read aloud ACTS 8:25–40

The Samaritans were despised and rejected by the Jewish people. They refused to associate with one another, yet the Holy Spirit welcomed them into Christ's kingdom as readily as the most devout Jew in Jerusalem. Philip's ministry in Samaria is the gateway for the spread of the gospel to the most unlikely of candidates. His obedience in taking the message to this people group resulted in the apostles beginning to fulfill the Great Commission of Christ to tell of Him to the world!

Read Acts 8:25–29.
Describe what the apostles did on their way back to Jerusalem.

Where does Philip go and why?

Who did Philip encounter?

Where was he coming from, where was he going, and what was he doing?

Who spoke to Philip in verse 29? Who had spoken to him in verse 26?

It's interesting how Luke differentiates between the angel and the Holy Spirit in giving Philip his directives. For Philip to take the route the angel suggested meant heading into the middle of the desert. With no means of transportation, this could easily mean death. Once Philip obeyed this unexplainable request, he now became led solely by the Spirit. God is so merciful, isn't He? Asking Philip to head out to the middle of the desert was completely contrary to anything logical. Philip was an evangelist. Who would hear the message in the middle of the desert? Was he supposed to preach to the sand? After witnessing such revival in Samaria, I'm sure Philip was eager to go to another largely populated city to see what God might do there in the hearts of the people. But God sends him an angel telling him to head out into the middle of nowhere.

Now see verses 30 and 31. What did Philip ask the man, and what was the response?

Look at the incredible intricacy of God's timing. One seeking heart, one page of Scripture, and one willing servant of God resulted in the gospel being spread to an entire nation! God sent Philip completely out of his way to present the gospel to one solitary individual. If you feel like you are wandering all alone on a solitary path, remember this Ethiopian eunuch. God knows the path that you take and He is ready and willing to come to your aid, bringing you a message of life!

When you read that God will go out of His way to rescue one lone soul, how does that make you feel?

I can't help but contrast the Ethiopian's search for God versus Simon's requests. Simon requested to know and understand God's power for his own selfish gain. This eunuch's request to understand God resulted in the truth of the gospel being brought to another continent. When you open up the pages of Scripture in search of greater understanding of your Savior, do you anticipate the ripple effects of your searching? Do you expect God to have a plan in place to take that truth that He is giving you to impact people beyond your own world? Or do we open the Scriptures only hoping for comfort and answers to our own problems and concerns? Do we obsess over receiving direction for our own worries of life and never open our hearts and minds to the limitless possibilities of our obedience to and application of God's Word?

The Ethiopian held a deep desire to know and understand Scripture. God was about to give Him a taste of just how incredible He is!

Let's read Acts 8:23–35.
To whom do you think the passage quoted refers?

What question did the eunuch ask and what was Philip's answer?

What had Jesus done on the road to Emmaus in Luke 24:26–27?

This searching soul did not have the Holy Spirit to guide him to understand all truth. But God sent Philip to him, and his eyes were opened. I picture him sitting in his chariot reading this passage aloud over and over again with all manner of inflections and emphasis trying to determine what it meant, all to no avail as it still made no sense to him. Yet somehow he knew there was a significant truth buried within the words and he sought to unearth it.

Along comes Philip, who explains it in great detail. God saw his seeking heart and led him to salvation through His Son. The love of God is limitless! We see Philip obediently following the Holy Spirit to places unexplainable.

How did this Ethiopian eunuch respond to Philip's explanation, according to Acts 8:36?

Notice Philip did not doubt for one second that the salvation of Jesus was available to this man as readily as to his Jewish brethren. God gave Philip the perfect set-up to share the gospel with this man. Do we expect God to do the same for us with the people whom we are called to share? Personally I tend to discount their possible interest and feel like I would be annoying or burdening them to go into a long explanation of who Jesus is, but maybe I need to trust that today could be their day of salvation and that God has prepared their heart to receive it!

Have you ever been in a situation where you heard the gospel randomly shared with someone and they readily accepted it?

When was the last time you heard a story like this? Describe the circumstances.

See verses 38–39. What happened to Philip after he baptized the eunuch? What about the eunuch?

The history of the Christian church in Ethiopia has traditionally been traced back to this eunuch. As John MacArthur puts it, "Through this man, a high official in the court of the Ethiopian queen, the gospel would first penetrate the souls of the great African continent."[18] One searching soul, one portion of Scripture, and one faithful follower brought the message of salvation to an entire nation.

What impact could God make through you with what you studied today?

With whom could you share the gospel today—no matter how random?

God's eye is on one searching soul waiting to understand Him. Maybe you are the one God intends to send with the explanation. Being used of God to bring someone into the family of God is pretty unexplainable.

WEEK 6 | DAY 5
SLOW OF HEART

Please read aloud ACTS 8:25–40

can't wait to talk with Philip when I get to heaven! How did he discern God's desire to spread the message of the gospel to the Gentiles? Or did he not actually discern it at all, he just merely obeyed the prompting of the Spirit one step at a time and didn't overthink things? Did God reveal it to him the moment he stepped into the Ethiopian's chariot?

I also wonder if Philip had been acquainted with Jesus while He had walked the earth. When did Philip first hear of Jesus and accept Him as the Messiah? Philip's faith and obedience to God appears outrageous at times—definitely unexplainable!

Maybe the Holy Spirit did reveal to Philip what He was doing precisely at that moment, by leading both he and the eunuch to this particular portion of Scripture. The eunuch was reading from Isaiah 53 where Isaiah prophesied regarding the suffering servant.

What did Isaiah say about this servant in Isaiah 52:15?

How could that apply to this Ethiopian eunuch?

What else did Isaiah say in Isaiah 56:1–8?

Maybe the passage in Isaiah from which the eunuch read was a lesson for Philip as much as it was the means of salvation for the eunuch. It is plausible that one of the first Gentile converts was a eunuch! Maybe God needed to make it that obvious to allow Philip to overcome some preconceived ideas. I don't know about you, but this gives me great hope. I can be a real knucklehead sometimes and miss what God is doing, but in His great patience and instruction He slowly clears my vision and reveals what He is doing. Yet I've often been ignorant of His plans for days, months, and years. In contrite confession I admit my failure to recognize His work and my resistance to His plans.

Just recently my husband and I had a sharp disagreement regarding a decision about his medical practice. For the first six years of its existence I helped him build and manage it. Right after I received the offer to write this study he wanted to hire a nurse practitioner. Doing so would require hours of work on my end to get someone hired, trained, credentialed; and then I'd have to follow up with hiring additional staff members to aid the new employee in scheduling and treating patients. I felt this decision was unfair and insensitive on his part, and I'll confess I wasn't very submissive about it. I could feel resentment growing in my heart. How was I supposed to handle this transition at work and write a book at the same time? It seemed impossible!

Through a series of events, God brought us the perfect nurse practitioner, promoted someone from within our practice to take over my role as practice manager, and provided a wonderful woman of God to work the front desk. While I had felt confined by this decision, God was actually bringing it about to free me to write. In the meantime, I had been a brat to my husband and I had failed to see what God was doing. I had some serious apologizing to do to both of them!

Have you ever missed what God was doing only to look back and wish you had behaved differently?

Where did the Spirit take Philip next (verse 40), and where did he eventually end up?

The city of Azotus formerly had been called Ashdod. It was one of the five city-states that had comprised the Philistine empire. The Israelites had held a long and bitter rivalry with the Philistines until they were finally defeated by David. Azotus came under Israel's control during the reign of Pompey and was under King Herod's jurisdiction. However, this city previously had been under pagan control for centuries. The population within Azotus would have been much more diverse than other places in Judea. No wonder the Spirit sent Philip there!

Where Philip eventually lands for good reveals the most about the Spirit's plans, however. At the end of his travels he returns to Caesarea Philippi. We discussed the significance of this place on Day 2 this week. It was in this city that Jesus revealed His plan to overthrow all pagan religion and reveal the truth of God to all people (recall Matthew 16:13–18). He not only revealed that plan but asserted that it would be fulfilled through His disciples. Peter would lead the charge. Yet so far it seems Philip is the only one on board. Both of these cities, Azotus and Caesarea Philippi, were inundated with pagan philosophies and religions. Yet these are the places to which Philip was sent.

Where are you willing to allow the Spirit to send you?

Have you ever gone to a place out of obedience to God even though it made no sense at the time or you could not see why God was leading you there? Share it with your group.

While we often want to see the end result of what God is doing, He often only reveals His plans to us one step at a time. Why do you think God chooses to operate in this manner?

Just because we cannot see where God is headed does not mean He is not leading. Often He asks us to take a step toward the unknown just to see if we will follow Him. It might look like a road to nowhere, but someone else's path to salvation just might be our own road to revelation. Follow Him!

unexplainable unity

WEEK 7 | DAY 1
MAY I INTRODUCE MYSELF?
Please read aloud ACTS 9:1-9

While Philip brought revival to Samaria, took the gospel to Africa via the Ethiopian eunuch, and continued to spread the gospel throughout Israel and Judea, Peter and John continued what Philip had started. The Great Commission's fulfillment had begun. The gospel had gone forth in Jerusalem, Judea, and Samaria and began to be spread to all the ends of the earth. Luke's narrative now shifts to highlight the process of how this begins to be fulfilled.

Of course, as we read previously, opposition arose. While all of these incredible things were happening throughout Israel, Jerusalem remained a hotbed for religious persecution of the early believers.

See Acts 9:1–2.
What has Saul been up do since we last saw him? What does he believe about the church?

What request did Saul make of the high priest in Acts 9:2?

Damascus was located 150 miles north of Jerusalem, and a large Jewish population resided there. Part of Syria, it was outside the borders of Israel, yet still under King Agrippa's jurisdiction. After Stephen's death, many believers presumably fled there, and in his zeal, Saul desired to bring them back to Jerusalem. Interestingly, his travels most likely led him directly through Samaria where immense revival was currently happening!

What term is used to describe the early believers in Acts 9:2?

How had Jesus described Himself in John 14:6?

Here we have Saul, expertly trained in the Scriptures, yet he completely missed the heart of God. Sobering! In a lot of ways, Saul and Simon the Sorcerer had much in common.

Both sought man's praise.

How did Saul later describe himself in Galatians 1:10?

Religion was the tool they used for personal gain and significance.

What did Saul say in Philippians 3:4–7?

They sought to serve God in a way that benefitted themselves. They sought God for what they could *get from Him*, not out of thankfulness *for what He had already done.*

How have you seen people try to use God in the ways listed above?

However, I also believe there was a level of deep sincerity within Saul. While his efforts were misguided, his determined obedience to the law still heralds a shred of nobility. As we dig further into our story, Jesus Himself speaks of Saul's split conscience in chasing after his own religious ambition with his nagging doubts that he was doing the right thing.

Read Acts 9:3–6.
Describe what happened.

What question did Saul ask, and what answer did he receive?

What was he told to do?

Can you imagine Saul's confusion in this moment? I often wonder at what point Saul actually surrendered his heart to Jesus. Was it at this very moment, or not until he had some time to process the encounter? Saul was a highly respected, brilliant young scholar. It's not easy for a person like that to suddenly realize he was wrong. And in the case of Stephen's stoning—dead wrong.

Interestingly, Saul's vision contained similarities with Ezekiel's.

Compare the two visions; see Ezekiel 1:4, 25, 28 in light of Acts 9:3–4.

Saul answers the voice with the word "Lord." The Greek word is *kurios*, meaning "mighty one."[19] This term was used for those who held authority in civil government and also for divine beings.[20] Saul is not yet recognizing the deity of Christ. His failure to recognize the person of Jesus cannot be pinpointed. First of all, Jesus' appearance consisted of His glorified state, not as He had appeared in human form.

Paul later likens it to the "glory of the Lord" (see 2 Corinthians 4:6). Second, we don't know if Paul actually saw the form of Jesus Himself or merely a blinding light with a voice emanating from within it.

Jesus tells Saul that by persecuting believers he is actually persecuting Jesus Himself. Christ's identification with His church is an indivisible oneness. Whatever victimization has been done to one of His children has been directly done to Him; the shame, guilt, anger, and horror experienced by the victim are also suffered by the Savior. Rather than run away from Him in our emotional turmoil, this truth ought to spur us into the arms of the only one who truly is able to understand.

Recall one of the most difficult or painful seasons or events in your life.

Now read Hebrews 4:14–16. Summarize your reaction to this passage:

Write verse 16 here:

While Saul just experienced the beautiful light of the throne of grace, his traveling companions remained in the dark.

Describe what they saw and heard in Acts 9:7:

We don't know why Saul's companions could not discern the words Jesus had spoken. It's possible that it's because the message was only intended for Saul.

Describe Saul's continuation of his journey in Acts 9:8:

Zealous and arrogant Saul, leading the charge in the persecution of the church, suddenly becomes stopped in his tracks and utterly dependent on his traveling companions to take even one step.

Has God ever stopped you in your tracks before? Describe the circumstance and what God taught you during this time. Maybe it's a situation you are facing today.

What did Saul do as a result of this vision according to Acts 9:9?

We can infer that for the next three days Saul devoted himself solely to prayer (Acts 9:11), since fasting was often accompanied by prayer. Personally, I think Saul's prayers consisted first of confession—to his pride, stubbornness, ignorance, and of course his horrible actions in persecuting believers. I also believe he intensely sought Jesus for understanding of His Person and His mission. He waited for Jesus to tell him what to do. Remember, Saul was a man of action.

When God steps in and frustrates your plans, goals, or ambitions, what types of prayer do you predominantly present to Jesus?

Why would it be important for Saul to truly understand the person of Jesus before being told what He wanted him to do?

Close your study today by reexamining Philippians 3:10 in the Amplified version:

[For my determined purpose is] that I may know Him [that I may progressively become more deeply and intimately acquainted with Him, perceiving and recognizing and understanding the wonders of His Person more strongly and more clearly], and that I may in that same way come to know the power outflowing from His resurrection [which it exerts over believers], and that I may so share His sufferings as to be continually transformed [in spirit into His likeness even].

Circle the aspect of this verse that most describes your heart's desire toward Jesus.

That, my friend, is a prayer worth praying. It is also a prayer Jesus loves to answer!

Read those verses out loud as a prayer to Him today. Ask Him to make this your "determined purpose."

"FAITHFULL" OBEDIENCE

Please read aloud ACTS 9:10–19

We ended yesterday with Saul hobbling blindly into Damascus, led by his traveling companions. Upon his arrival he fasted and prayed, processing all that had just occurred. Little did Saul know, Jesus has also appeared to another man.

To whom did Jesus appear in Acts 9:10 and by what title did Luke refer to him?

How did this man answer Jesus?

What did Jesus tell him to do in Acts 9:11?

This faithful servant held no particular title of authority within the early church. He was simply a follower of Jesus. When Jesus appeared to him, he recognized Him instantly and also indicated he was ready to obey. Did you notice he responded with eagerness even before he knew what Jesus was going to ask of him? Ananias's response describes a Philippians 3:10 person—he had resolved in his heart to obey God no matter what.

Often we want God to give us some assignment to complete, but God usually works through an opposite chain of events. First He asks, "Have you determined to know Me and understand My ways?" and *then* He hands out specific assignments. In God's syllabus, we depend on the character and faithfulness of God to accomplish His plans, not our own understanding of our abilities, inherent risks, or possible difficulties and setbacks. None of those things are of concern to God. His only concern is our desire to have a heart willing to obey Him. He takes care of the rest.

Maybe instead of praying for God to reveal His assignment for us, the prayer should be for a heart that's resolved to obey Him no matter what He may ask us to do. Our focus should not be on what He reveals, but rather on who the Revealer is!

Read Acts 9:12–14.
What did Jesus tell Ananias, and how did he respond?

Even faithful and obedient Ananias wrestled with Jesus' directives. No wonder God takes such care to ready our hearts before calling us to work. Jesus gave specific directions to Ananias so he could not back out due to fear. God told him the exact location where he would find Saul. Without these specific instructions, Ananias could have wandered into a local synagogue and asked, "Anybody seen Saul here?" From there he could have meandered over to the market place and inquired of a couple of merchants, "Have you happened to come across a Pharisee from Jerusalem named Saul today? No? Okay, thanks, see ya." From there he could have justified himself to the Lord. "I looked for him roundabout, but to no avail; I wasn't able to locate him!" Halfhearted obedience.

Have I ever been guilty of this! Let's give it some modern day analogies. God prompted you to seek reconciliation with someone, so you offered a halfhearted apology. God pricked your heart to serve in a particular capacity, but you showed up late and ill-prepared. God continued to press you toward a particular area of obedience, so you did for a couple of days, then offered excuses why you were unable to continue. Done, done, and done. I've done them all. At which point God reminds me, "Child, this isn't about your behavior as much as it's about your heart! I'm not asking you to do these things because doing them works out some magic result in your life—I'm asking you to do them because I want to know that your heart's deepest desire is to obey Me!"

What is Jesus telling us in Luke 6:46 and John 15:5 and 10?

Paraphrase Jesus' response in your own words. See Acts 9:15–16.

Jesus assured Ananias that the horror Saul had inflicted on the early believers had not gone unnoticed by Jesus. Saul's suffering, however, would serve an incredible purpose in glorifying Christ and advancing the gospel. "Don't worry about justice, Ananias. I have a plan and a purpose in choosing Saul." I think as Christians we often hold back from obeying the Lord because we feel that it might deny the evildoer the justice we feel is due them.

Interestingly, the name Ananias means "grace." In other words, "Lord, are you certain this is a man to whom I am to extend your grace?" When the answer was "Go!" he obeyed.

Read Acts 9:17–19.
What two things did Ananias do for Saul?

What happened once Ananias did these things?

What two things did Saul do?

Then where did Saul go?

I believe Saul's moment of conversion happened in this interaction with Ananias. During these three days, I believe Saul was slowly coming to the realization of who Jesus is. However, it was before Ananias that he publicly confessed his desire to submit his life to Jesus as Lord.

Later Saul (Paul) explained one's moment of conversion in Romans 10:9. Write the verse here:

Look carefully at Acts 9:17 again. By what title did Ananias address Saul?

I love this! Can you imagine walking up to this man, a murderer of fellow believers, and calling him your brother? Ananias was indeed a man of much grace! Notice also with what certainty Ananias addresses Jesus' lordship and Saul's commitment to it. "He sent me to bring you the Holy Spirit." This is Scripture's first mention of a disciple anointing someone with the Holy Spirit. At Pentecost the Spirit fell independently. In Samaria Peter and John laid their hands on the people for the Spirit to come days after their conversion. Now a non-apostle lays hands on a future apostle for the Holy Spirit to be given. One thing for sure, we cannot put the Holy Spirit in a box when it comes to His ways!

Just think if Ananias had been unwilling to obey. He could have said to the Lord, "I'm sorry, Jesus. I just don't have it in me. Send someone else to do it." Or he could have said, "Jesus, that's just too risky. I still have little kids at home to worry about. I can't put my life in jeopardy right now. Ask me in a few more years when it's the right season." Saul's introduction to the believers in Damascus had come through Ananias. He would have missed out on the miracle of seeing Saul's sight restored. Who knows how the Holy Spirit might have been given to Saul in the event Ananias refused to go?

None of us know what Jesus may call us to do. All we know is that He asks us to make our hearts ready. That comes from a resolve to obey—no matter what. When we know our heart is not ready, He promises us He will make it so. Shall we ask Him to make us ready? Close today with your own time of prayer. Ask the Lord to search your heart. Ask Him to make you into a person full of grace, ready and willing to obey. Ask Him to make your life unexplainable!

A LITTLE ENCOURAGEMENT

Please read aloud ACTS 9:20–31

Can you even imagine the reaction when Ananias ushered Saul into the crowd of believers? A hush must have fallen over everyone, nervous fidgeting, mothers' arms instinctively encircling their children and holding them close. "It's Saul . . . the murderer . . . why is Ananias bringing him in here?" What was Saul feeling? Shame? Guilt? Embarrassment? Was he even able to lift his head to look his new family of believers in the face?

After the initial shock, they welcomed him. Luke tells us that Saul stayed with the believers in Damascus for several days. Saul must have been overwhelmed by their love and unity. He could hardly contain himself.

Read Acts 9:20–25.
What did Saul immediately begin to do?

How did the people of Damascus respond to Saul?

How does Luke describe Saul's ability to preach the gospel?

What plan did the Jews concoct?

Why did their plan fail?

Many readers of Acts might assume here that Saul went directly to Jerusalem. But if we look at Galatians 1:11–24 we see instead that Saul took a different journey.

Fill out the timeline of Saul's travels according to the Galatians passage, noting especially verses 17–21.

For I would have you know, brothers, that the gospel that was preached by me is not man's gospel. For I did not receive it from any man, nor was I taught it, but I received it through a revelation of Jesus Christ. For you have heard of my former life in Judaism, how I persecuted the church of God violently and tried to destroy it. And I was advancing in Judaism beyond many of my own age among my people, so extremely zealous was I for the traditions of my fathers. But when he who had set me apart before I was born, and who called me by his grace, was pleased to reveal his Son to me, in order that I might preach him among the Gentiles, I did not immediately consult with anyone; nor did I go up to Jerusalem to those who were apostles before me, but I went away into Arabia, and returned again to Damascus.

Then after three years I went up to Jerusalem to visit Cephas and remained with him fifteen days. But I saw none of the other apostles except James the Lord's brother. (In what I am writing to you, before God, I do not lie!) Then I went into the regions of Syria and Cilicia. And I was still unknown in person to the churches of Judea that are in Christ. They only were hearing it said, "He who used to persecute us is now preaching the faith he once tried to destroy." And they glorified God because of me.

Paul's testimony is unexplainable. His conversion miraculous, his transformation astounding, and his obedience inspiring. Paul became as zealous in his explanation of Jesus as he had been for his Jewish traditions and the Law. Luke slips in a phrase here to emphasize Paul's boldness. While Peter explained Jesus as the suffering servant and Stephen emphasized him to be the Promised One spoken of by Moses, Paul uses a **new** term to explain Jesus' identity. What is it? See 9:20.

This name for Jesus—Son of God—was going to upset the Jewish leaders; it was also going to create a big problem among the Romans. This title did not merely grant Jesus civic authority, it also granted him spiritual authority. He was now on par with the Roman gods. No wonder everywhere Paul went he either incited revival or a riot!

After three years of preparation in Arabia and then traveling to Syria and Cilicia, Paul finally returns to Jerusalem.

> Saul was a Roman citizen. It was common for Jewish men in the first century who held Roman citizenship to have their Hebrew name as well as a Greek name. Once Saul begins his ministry to the Gentiles, he begins to predominantly use his Greek name: Paul. His letters to the churches in our New Testament are collectively referred as the Pauline Epistles.

Read Acts 9:26–31.
How did the disciples respond to Paul's return?

Who came and met Paul and where did he take him?

What proof did he cite as to the veracity of Paul's conversion?

What did Paul do? (verse 28)

From where did Paul's greatest opposition arise?

What did the disciples decide to do as a result?

What five things resulted in Paul's departure?

Here we are introduced to a second man courageous enough to offer grace to the undeserving: Barnabas. His name means "son of encouragement." Paul's life demonstrated the truth of his conversion. No doubt Paul could have become immensely discouraged when the disciples spurned him. His own guilt and shame over his persecution of the church could be enough to incapacitate him. Now Jesus returned him to the scene of his crimes, and the rejection by other Christians indeed must have slain him in the depths of his heart.

So God sent an encourager. In his initial shame at misunderstanding Jesus, he was sent grace in Ananias. Now in his discouragement, he is sent the son of encouragement. Oh, how good is our God! He sends us exactly what we need when we need it! It is also important to note that neither Ananias nor Barnabas held significant roles of leadership within the church. They were fellow brethren, ready to serve whomever God sent their way. In crucial moments in Paul's life, they both played pivotal roles in spurring him on to the next step in God's plan for him.

Who has been an Ananias to you when you needed a touch of grace?

To whom have you been an Ananias?

Who has been a Barnabas to you when you needed encouragement?

To whom have you been a Barnabas?

We all need grace and encouragement at times, don't we? Just think if Barnabas had been unwilling to take Paul to the apostles. Quite possibly a harmful schism could have occurred between the Jewish believers and the Gentile converts under Paul's ministry. Barnabas's willingness to encourage Paul unified the soon-to-be-widening church. How often we underestimate the ripple effects of what a simple act of encouragement can accomplish!

Knowledge of Paul's conversion flooded the believers with fresh energy and excitement. Their former archenemy now began to be persecuted for his zeal for Jesus. Unexplainable! However, these believers were also tired. The persecution of the early church had been relentless. Paul's return to Jerusalem began to stir up even more trouble. He had to go. So they sent him back to his hometown of Tarsus. Remember, God had made it clear that Paul was His chosen instrument to go to the Gentiles. His ministry did not belong in Jerusalem. For an additional seven to eight years, Paul would continue to undergo more preparation.

After Paul's departure, the early church finally experienced a season of rest. During this time, Luke informs us that the church grew in numbers as they were "walking in the fear of the Lord."

Look carefully again at Acts 9:31. Fill in the blanks:

_____ in the fear of the Lord and in _____
of the Holy Spirit.

What do you think those two phrases mean: encouraged/comforted by the Holy Spirit and living/walking in the fear of the Lord?

Describe people in your church you feel exhibit those two characteristics.

Why do you suppose those two characteristics would result in church growth?

If we desire to increase those characteristics in our own lives, what are some practical steps we could employ?

Going back to Ananias and Barnabas again, I believe that seeking opportunities to extend grace and encouragement to others brings about these particular characteristics into our lives. When we seek to encourage others, the Holy Spirit encourages us. When we live or walk in the fear of the Lord, we intentionally offer grace to others because we become exceedingly mindful of how undeserving we are of the grace we have already received. Little did Ananias and Barnabas know how immensely their faithful obedience would impact Christ's kingdom through Paul.

Yesterday we emphasized how our outward obedience is a mirror pointing back to what is hidden within our heart. Our ability to serve others faithfully is also a window to the depths of our heart. A willingness to reach out to someone else with no explanation other than feeling prompted by God is completely unexplainable! When you follow in obedience, you probably will have no idea the impact you make. But the Holy Spirit will know, and He will encourage you in return.

WEEK 7 | DAY 4
LYDDA, SHARON, AND JOPPA

Please read aloud ACTS 9:32–43

Today we are going to look at the beautiful tapestry of the theme of the believers' work weaving together. Remember where Philip went after his encounter with the Ethiopian? The Spirit transported him to Azotus, and from there he traveled up the coast to Caesarea. On his way, he preached the gospel in all the towns and villages through which he traveled, such as Lydda and Joppa. While Luke asserts Paul's incredible apologetic skills in preaching the gospel, he now shifts Peter into more of a pastoral role. We see Peter revisiting the believers with whom Philip had shared the good news of the gospel.

Read Acts 9:32–35.
While Philip was evangelizing and Paul was debating, what was Peter doing?

What did Peter tell Aeneas, and what happened as a result?

How did the residents of these towns respond?

So Philip planted the seeds of the gospel message and established groups of believers in Lydda and Joppa, and then Peter came to harvest yet more souls through the working of miracles. Both men working together, exercising different gifts, spread the message of salvation among the people. This is another picture of what was emphasized yesterday through the working of Ananias, Barnabas, and Paul.

Have you ever taken the time to discover your own spiritual gift(s)? Paul asserts that everyone who has chosen to follow Christ has been given a spiritual gift for the building up of the church. What does Paul say about spiritual gifts? Refer to 1 Corinthians 12:1–4 and circle all below.

- *it is important that we understand them*

- *it is the Spirit inside of us that recognizes Jesus as Lord*

- *spiritual gifts come from different spirits*

- *all spiritual gifts come from the Holy Spirit*

- *there are different types of gifts*

- *everyone has all of the gifts*

- *spiritual gifts are for our own enjoyment*

- *spiritual gifts are to be used to benefit others*

If you do not know what your own spiritual gifts are, you may decide in your small group to ask your pastor or ministry leader for a spiritual gifts inventory to help you discover how God has equipped you to build up your church.

> To learn more about spiritual gifts and for information on taking a spiritual gifts inventory, see Deeper Discoveries at ericawiggenhorn.com.

As we'll see in this next portion of Acts, the Spirit can manifest Himself in both practical and supernatural ways.

Read Acts 9:36–43.
Who was Tabitha and what was she known for?

What happened to her?

Describe the widows' show-and-tell for Peter. Why do you think they did this?

What did Peter do for Tabitha and what resulted?

Tabitha probably had the spiritual gift of "service" or "helps." She took her ability to sew and put it to good use. I doubt she sewed in isolation, however. These precious widows grieved her absence. They still had the clothing she provided; it was Tabitha who was dear to their hearts. I imagine she encouraged these widows and showed them love in both word and deed. Women like Tabitha are the heartbeat of the church. Women who cook meals when someone is ill, mop floors, wash clothes, stock pantries, and whistle while they work are true gifts from God.

I recall when our son was born. He had to stay the first week of his little life in the hospital. Because his birth mother lived on the other side of Detroit, he had been born near where she lived, which was quite far from our home on the northwest side of the city. After being away from home for several days and up for several nights, you can imagine the tremendous gratitude I felt when I came home to a slow cooker full of warm food and a refrigerator and pantry stocked with meals for the week. My friends had even gotten diapers and formula! Talk about feeling loved!

We love to share stories of amazing miracles like Peter just performed in Aeneas's life, but the Tabitha stories are those most worth telling. The Spirit can sweep in and find anyone willing to do something spectacular for God. It takes a special person willing to be a Tabitha.

Who do you know you would consider a Tabitha? What makes her or them so?

When has someone been a Tabitha to you personally?

Who do you know who could really use a Tabitha right now—a widow, a single mom, someone who is ill? What could you do to be a Tabitha in their life?

After Peter performed these miracles in Lydda and Joppa, where did he go?

We could assume Luke drops in the fact that Simon was a tanner merely for identification purposes, but there is more significance to his occupation. A tanner was a lowly trade in the world of the Jews. According to Levitical law, Jewish men were not to touch dead animals, and tanners cured and created goods from leather. Therefore, tanners were perpetually unclean due to their line of work. Within this tiny detail Luke foreshadows the extension of grace over the law that is about to come next.

YOUR NECK OF THE WOODS

Please read aloud ACTS 9

Spread out over hundreds of miles, various disciples and apostles busied them-selves with the work of the Lord. All separate, yet somehow interconnected, largely unaware of their impact in God's grander plan. Surely we will marvel at the unexplainable intricacies of God's work through His faithful followers when we are able to see the final picture. This week's emphasis shifts much more to the lay disciples than the powerhouse apostles or earth-shaking Paul. Luke slows down and introduces us to faithful believers who held no special titles or responsibilities within the early church. He ushered these normally behind-the-scenes folks center stage, spotlighting their indispensable contribution to the spread of the gospel.

Luke's intentions in bringing Ananias, Barnabas, Simon, and Tabitha into focus were to encourage ordinary folks like you and me, people who faithfully carry out our daily tasks hoping to make an impact, encouraging a friend or lightening the load of someone weighed down by the circumstances of life. We aren't performing miraculous signs and wonders like Peter, nor traveling all over the known world leading thousands to Christ like Philip, but what we do *matters*. And Peter and Philip could not do what they did without people like Simon, who opened his home, and Tabitha, who cared for others after the preaching was over and every-one went home.

If God were to call you to serve Him in any particular way, what would you hope it might be?

Is there an area of your life where you feel you make a difference? If so, what is it, and why do you feel that way?

Is there a stirring in your heart of how you could possibly serve in some capacity? If so, what is keeping you from moving forward?

During most seasons of life, our area of service that is most time-consuming will be within our families. Young children require nearly all our time and energy, and there is no more important work than pouring into the gifts that God has given us in our children! I think it is important though, to maintain a proper perspective in regard to caring for our home and rearing our children. One of the biggest ways to teach our children to be others-centered is to allow them to see us meeting the needs of those around us.

A dear friend of mine balances this better than anyone I know. She homeschools her three children, all while inviting other children over when moms need a break, cooking extra food to deliver to someone in need, or having her children help her bake brownies for others just to say, "I care!" She tailors her service around the raising of her children. The remarkable thing is how her children have become so others-centered in the process. Often when they are at my home, they will walk into the kitchen and ask me, "Ms. Erica, is there something I can help you with?" Not many six- and eight-year-olds do that, but my friend's kids do, because they see their mama doing it day in and day out in the lives of others.

What advice would you give to a mother of young children on how to balance/combine serving in the church with effectively discipling her children?

What advice would you give to a woman who has already raised her children on how to balance/combine serving young mothers in the church with other areas of ministry?

Thinking back to the many people we met this week:
How could you use your home to build up the church like Simon?

How could you use a skill to build up the church like Tabitha?

What do you see as some of the biggest needs in your community?

What are some of the biggest needs in your church?

The opportunities are endless. We don't have to think about doing something big, we just need to be open to doing something. As long as we're living, God is still working on us, and He wants to work through us. It's the humble, obedient, faithful, behind-the-scenes folks who are truly unexplainable. The spotlight's on, the stage is ready, and your audience of One is watching. Who could you serve today?

our unexplainable God

WEEK 8 | DAY 1
NOT FAR OFF

Please read aloud ACTS 10:1–8

At the end of Acts 9, Peter's miracles resulted in many Jews coming to faith in Christ. Luke also intimated Peter's willingness to extend grace over the law by staying in a tanner's home. Today's passage opens wide the floodgates of grace in the city of Caesarea (note that this is a different city than Caesarea Philippi, where Peter proclaimed the great statement of who Jesus is).

Read today's passage aloud from Acts 10:1–8 to help set the scene.
What was Cornelius by occupation?

Describe Cornelius and his family.

Caesarea was a thriving city that housed a section of the Roman garrison. Trusted and skilled soldiers were stationed there. A port city built up by Herod the Great, traders there paid hefty taxes to disperse goods from their ships onto the mainland. The city boasted great wealth.

Here we meet Cornelius, a Roman Gentile, well-versed in Roman paganism, yet worships the God of Israel. A devout follower, he practices the Jewish prayer ritual of praying three times a day.

Read Acts 10:3–8.
What happened to Cornelius in verse 3?

How did he react?

How did the angel respond to him? What was Cornelius to do?

What action did Cornelius take?

Cornelius must have been a pretty incredible guy. Not only had his character affected his family, but it also spilled over into the hundred soldiers under his command. Cornelius is described as devout, generous, and God-fearing. His faith consisted of both belief and deed, since he not only ritually practiced his religion; he also lived it out practically.

His post-vision actions demonstrate these characteristics. Immediately after the vision, he gathers a trusted soldier and two servants to head to Joppa. Meanwhile, faith-filled Peter is in Joppa and has just raised Tabitha from the dead. As a result, many Jews came to faith in Jesus. Peter remains in Joppa for a time to equip this burgeoning church.

Just as the location of Caesarea plays an important role within Luke's tale, so does Joppa. Record what happened in Jonah 1:1–3:

God called Jonah to go preach to the Gentiles in Ninevah, but instead of obeying, he boarded a ship at Joppa, which was headed to Tarsus, to run away from his assignment. After he was thrown overboard and swallowed and spit up by a giant fish, God calls him a second time to go to this Gentile nation. This time Jonah obeys God, but when the Ninevites repent of their sin and turn to the Lord, Jonah becomes angry with God at His compassion.

Now Peter is in Joppa. Will he obey God and go to the Gentiles, or will he run away? Interestingly, Paul is currently in Tarsus, and he will be the ultimate missionary to the Gentile nations.

Cornelius has never even heard of Peter before. We know Philip was possibly in Caesarea by now, but most likely preached predominantly to the Greek Jews. Cornelius had not yet heard the gospel and he would not have been welcomed into a Jewish synagogue in Caesarea. A seeker of God, yet unable to fit into any of the communities in which God was worshiped. So God sent the church to him!

Can you think of a person or a subgroup of people who may feel uncomfortable worshiping in a traditional church setting? What might be a practical way to bring the church to them?

I remember fearing for my sisters in the prison yard once they were released. Their entire worship experience had consisted of "prison church." No one there judged their tattoos or questioned if they were really saved, since the only Christians they knew were those of us who brought Christ into the prison yard and who accepted them unconditionally. Once they were released, I expected that they would meet Christians who would reject them simply because of how they looked or because they had served time. Instead of experiencing Christ's love within the walls of the church, they could experience shame and condemnation. Likewise, a devout Jew in Caesarea would not have welcomed Cornelius into their home to explain the ways of God to him. It went against everything they had been taught.

It makes me wonder how Cornelius had come to know the God of Israel in the first place. Where had he first been introduced to Him? Luke doesn't tell us, but Cornelius was obviously quite open about it. I'm not sure how that all jived with his Roman cohorts. It definitely contradicted emperor worship, which would become increasingly popular in a short time within Rome. The lesson of Cornelius is the same as that of the Ethiopian eunuch: every individual holds equal importance in the heart of God. There is not a soul on earth whom God does not love. This is hard for us to fathom.

How do you suppose Cornelius may have been exposed to the God of Israel?

Do you know people who have stepped away from the church because of past hurts or experiences within the church walls?

What are some practical ways to minister to these people and encourage them to reenter the body of believers?

So Peter sits in Joppa. Will he go? It's going to take something pretty unexplainable to convince him he's supposed to go to Caesarea. But then again, we have a pretty unexplainable God!

THE ENDS OF THE EARTH

Please read aloud ACTS 10:9–20

Read this beautiful passage aloud before beginning today's study. These verses show the compassionate heart of God to reach the lost.

The scene today rapidly shifts from Caesarea to Joppa. Luke opens the curtain, emphasizing Peter's Jewish heritage.

What was Peter doing in Acts 10:9?

Peter headed up to the roof to pray. Roofs functioned then much like patios do today, serving as an extension of the home. While Peter is praying on the roof in the city of Joppa, he is about to be mentally transported far beyond the physical boundaries of Israel.

What happened to Peter while he was on the roof?

The word "trance" or "visionary state" is the Greek word *ekstasis*. Our English equivalent is "ecstasy," meaning "the mind for a time is carried out and beyond itself, great astonishment and amazement."[21]

What did Peter see?

The four corners of the earth symbolized the entire world. The sheet full of animals represented the totality of all living creatures on earth.

What did the voice tell Peter, and how did he respond?

Peter's answer was adamant! "I will have none of it, Lord!" Peter strictly continued to follow Jewish law and customs despite the grace he had received through Jesus Christ. A similar conversation had occurred hundreds of years prior between God and one of His prophets.

What did God tell Ezekiel to do? (Ezekiel 4:9–13)

How did Ezekiel answer Him? (verse 14)

How did God respond to Ezekiel? (verse 15)

How did God respond to Peter in Acts 10:15–16?

What had Jesus taught in Matthew 15:10–11?

What did Peter do in Matthew 15:15 after Jesus taught this?

How did Jesus answer in Matthew 15:16–20?

To what region did Jesus travel next according to verse 21?

Immediately after Jesus taught about eating unclean foods, He took His disciples to a Gentile region. Once there He commended a Canaanite woman for her faith. In fact, there are only three recorded instances in the Gospels when Jesus commends people for their faith: Mary of Bethany when she anoints His feet (Mark 14:9), the Canaanite (Syrophoenician) woman in Sidon, and a Roman centurion. Hmmm, that sounds familiar—what was Cornelius's occupation again? (See Matthew 8:1–10.)

Read Acts 10:17–23.
How does Luke describe Peter's understanding of this vision?

As Peter is pondering this vision, what happens?

What did the Holy Spirit tell Peter?

What did the men say to Peter?

What did Peter do next?

We have to put this all in perspective. First, a Roman soldier rattling your gate generally meant trouble. Peter's initial reaction would be fear, thinking he was under arrest. Second, not only did Jewish men not eat the food of the Gentiles, they surely would not invite them into their home. Dating back to the law of Moses, Gentiles were considered unclean, and to bring them into your home made your home unclean. In our Western world of "tolerance" this makes us bristle, but we have to understand the culture. God called the people of Israel to live set apart.

So, while not explicitly stated, we assume Peter understood the vision because he invites this group of Gentile men into Simon's home. The walls of prejudice and division have already been broken down between the Jews and the Samaritans. They are now about to be destroyed between the Jews and the Gentiles.

Who did Peter take along with him to Caesarea?

That would be some mission trip! These unnamed brothers demonstrated even greater faith than Peter, in my estimation. They had not received a vision. The Holy Spirit had not specifically spoken to them. They merely had to take Peter's word for it that God was sending them to Cornelius's house. Imagine your pastor approaching you to travel to a war zone to meet with an enemy combatant because God had given him a vision to go tell him about Jesus. That is the kind of faith we're talking about here!

If you were one of the people sent to accompany Peter on this mission, how might you have felt?

Do you think you would have willingly gone with Peter, or tried to back out?

Has God ever prompted you to do something that possibly could have been dangerous? If so, how did you overcome your fear?

No wonder Peter needed to receive such strong confirmation from the Lord to follow this course of action! He was putting himself and other believers in possible danger by obeying this directive. Well, these faith-filled nameless believers are about to witness something so unexplainable you would have to see it with your own eyes to believe it! After it was all said and done, I am sure they were most grateful they followed Peter in blind faith. Sometimes we have to take steps in the darkness before God can reveal His glorious light. This is one of the unexplainable ways of God.

Deeper Discoveries discusses heavenly visions at ericawiggenhorn.com.

WEEK 8 | DAY 3
NOW I SEE!

Please read aloud ACTS 10:21–35

We ended yesterday with Peter doing something previously unexplainable: *he invited Gentile men into his home*. Deeply immersed in Jewish culture, Peter still could not grasp Jesus' directive to include all people in His kingdom. When Jesus spoke of all nations, Peter understood it to mean, "Jewish people in all nations." His upbringing caused him to interpret the words of Jesus into his own understanding. (While we should not impose our contemporary understanding of cultural bias on Peter, we can take a lesson from his experience.) Though we would not readily admit this to ourselves, I believe we have a tendency to do the same thing today—turn something to our own interpretation.

Well, at least I will confess that I do. I can quickly form an opinion of someone based entirely on how they're dressed, what type of vehicle they drive, or how they carry themselves. I hate to admit that, but if I'm honest with myself, it's true.

Pretty hypocritical, isn't it? I'm completely putting myself out there in writing this, because I know someone is going to email me with a directive to bring Christmas cookies to someone I've unfairly judged. How do you balance what realistically seems doable with the command to "Go and make disciples"? Consider my own neighbors. I can't share the gospel and disappear. I have to interact with them even when I may not feel like it or they're obviously annoyed with my efforts to be conversational. It's usually easier to be brave on paper, behind a computer screen, or on a social media platform than in real life.

What type of people do you see on a regular basis that you presume want nothing to do with Jesus?

A Roman centurion stationed in the Italian Regiment was no small potato. This guy had it made. He would be respected within his community and revered. It literally took divine intervention for Peter and the other believers to think they would be called to take him the gospel message.

Read Acts 10:24–36.
What did Peter encounter when he arrived in Cornelius's home?

What did Cornelius do when Peter came in, and what was Peter's response?

What did Peter tell the assembled crowd?

According to Acts 10:29, what is Peter still wondering?

What did Cornelius tell Peter?

Write out verse 33:

Suddenly it all makes sense. Peter now knows why he is here. God has called him to share the news of Jesus Christ to this group of Gentiles sitting before him. Peter finds this directive by the Holy Spirit incredulous! Definitely unexplainable! He never in a million years would have guessed this would be the result of a visit into a Gentile home.

What realization has dawned on Peter?

While the law forbade Jews from interacting with Gentiles, Moses, the chosen instrument of God to give the Law, understood this all along.

What does Moses say about Gentile nations in Deuteronomy 10:14–19?

What truths does Moses state about God?

This portion of Scripture is what Peter is quoting in Acts 10:34. Peter had probably recited these words on more occasions than he could count. Yet until this moment, he never fully understood them. This is the work of the Holy Spirit. He illuminates the Scriptures to us. While we may be familiar with what they say, He uses our human experience infused with His power to open our eyes to see their full meaning and application. Then suddenly we say like Peter, "Now I realize . . ."

For what did Paul specifically pray in Ephesians 1:17?

For what else did Paul pray for believers in Philippians 1:9?

What was Paul's purpose in all of these prayers according to Colossians 2:2? Identify four things:

Imagine praying for those four things over your loved ones: a mother's heart-cry for her children; a wife's quiet prayer for her husband; a prayer for an intimidating neighbor.

Paul also knew the Scriptures inside and out, but it took the work of the Holy Spirit to bring him to his "Now I see!" moment. Have you ever had a moment in your own life where suddenly a story or Scripture popped off the page at you in a moment of need? Write about it here:

On Day 1 of this study I asked you to answer the questions below regarding your own life. How have you seen the Holy Spirit work in Peter's and Paul's lives in the following ways throughout this study?

Record a time when God obviously directed their path through detours, closed doors, or opened ones.

Record a time when they unexplainably felt God's presence or power.

Record a passage of Scripture that jumped off the page and spoke to them in their time of need.

If you have your own experiences to now add after having reached this point in our study, please go back and add them to Day 1 now.

Throughout the story of Acts, we see the Holy Spirit's unlimited patience in revealing the truths of God to us. Peter and Paul's stubbornness to reexamine the truths of Scripture ought to encourage us. Most likely these men inherently knew the Bible in greater detail than any of us ever will, yet it took the work of the Holy Spirit to illuminate all of the implications and applications that it holds. This Wonderful Counselor never stopped working to reveal it to these men and He never stops working with us. Jesus promised that eventually we would be guided into *all* truth.

So just like Paul, we continue to pray for the Spirit to illuminate His Word to us. We continue to search the Scriptures asking for wisdom and revelation. We continue to ask the Holy Spirit to help us understand God more clearly. And we trust that in our moment of need, we will be able to say, just as Peter and Paul did, "Now I see!" And that will be unexplainable. I'll see you tomorrow. I suddenly feel the need to go bake some cookies.

AND SO SHALL YOU

Please read aloud ACTS 10:36–47

Before I ever speak to any group of women or even meet with an individual seeking advice, I always pray, "God, please give me the words You want me to say." On my own, I haven't got a thing. For one particular group, I felt my prayers returned with silence. So I thought maybe I should help God out a little by tossing up some suggestions to Him. Do you want me to share something about Ezekiel, Moses, or Elijah? Still silence. As the day loomed closer and I remained directionless, a shred of panic started to set in. I began to have a Moses moment as in Exodus 33, crying out to God, "If You're not going with me to do this, then please don't send me!" I imagine Peter experienced this traveling from Joppa to Caesarea. He had no idea what he was going to encounter when he arrived there. He was also clueless about why he was being sent.

It wasn't until he stood in front of the crowd in Cornelius's house that he suddenly knew what he was to do. When I finally arrived at the speaking engagement, I thought I had finally received an answer from God. Then my slides wouldn't work. I began to question if I had accepted this assignment outside of God's will. I started my talk without any visuals, praying for God to get me through it. Interestingly, about five minutes into the passage of Scripture, God changed my direction. All the illustrations and applications I thought I was to present were replaced with new ones. I walked out realizing that sometimes when we want God to do something unexplainable, we have to follow Him to places that have yet to be explained to us.

Read Acts 10:36–47.

What did Peter concede his audience had previously heard about?

Remember, Philip had traveled through Caesarea spreading the gospel already. Peter knew this news had reached his audience, but they had yet to fully grasp it.

What does Peter call himself? See verse 39.

How does Peter quantify Jesus' post-resurrection appearances?

What specifically had Peter been commanded to preach?

Why do you suppose Peter skipped over the prophets so briskly?

Describe what happened in verse 44. How did the Jewish believers react?

How did those assembled know that the Holy Spirit had been poured out?

What did Peter suggest should happen next?

Why do you suppose they asked Peter to remain with them?

What astonishes me most about the Holy Spirit is His personalization in each conversion story. In Lydda and Joppa, the people came to faith through miracles. In the home of Cornelius, these Gentiles came to faith purely through explanation. Peter did not use passages of Scripture, he merely explained the current events that these Roman citizens had seen and heard happening around them.

(And Cornelius already had the foundation of being God-fearing and "well spoken of by the whole Jewish nation.") Philip used Scripture to explain Jesus to the Ethiopian eunuch. Philip used a combination of both to bring the Samaritans to repentance. Peter *reasoned through the Scriptures* during Pentecost, as had Stephen before the Sanhedrin. While we didn't see the Holy Spirit bring anyone to belief through Stephen's sermon, we can infer from Paul's conversation with Jesus on the road to Damascus that a stirring had begun in Paul's heart and mind as to the truth of Stephen's testimony.

Imagine how Stephen's last words before his death must have echoed in Paul's mind and heart as he was later confronted on that dusty road by his Savior.

> "And falling to his knees he cried out with a loud voice, 'Lord, do not hold this sin against them.' And when he had said this, he fell asleep." (Acts 7:60)

In every instance the Spirit operated through different means and methods, yet accomplished the same goal: the revelation of Jesus as Lord! The Holy Spirit continuously keeps us guessing as to what He may do next. However, if there are two conversion stories that are most similar, it is the original outpouring of the Holy Spirit at Pentecost and His work in Cornelius's home. Look back at Acts 2:1–41 and record the similarities in the work of the Holy Spirit at Pentecost and in Cornelius's home.

THE SPIRIT AT PENTECOST

_____

_____

_____

_____

_____

_____

_____

THE SPIRIT AT CORNELIUS'S HOUSE

_____

_____

_____

_____

_____

_____

_____

Consider what you know about the relationship between the Jews and the Gentiles. Why might the Holy Spirit have worked in such a similar fashion in these two situations?

Why would it have been important for Peter not to have taken this trip alone, but to have other believers along with him?

Thinking back to the Samaritans' conversion and the necessity of Peter and John's arrival to dispense the Holy Spirit, why could Peter have been the first one to witness the outpouring of the Holy Spirit on the Gentiles rather than Paul, whom Jesus called His "chosen instrument" to go to the Gentile nations?

Think back to Jonah's call to preach to the people of Ninevah. Why might God have kept this mission hidden from Peter until his arrival?

When Jonathan and I first received the call that we had been chosen to adopt our son, we were over the moon! God had already blessed us with a beautiful daughter and now He was giving us a son. My husband and I could hardly contain our joy and anticipation. Over the next couple of months, walls were painted blue, baby clothes covered in baseballs and footballs were purchased, and dreams were built. Our family felt complete. Then things began to unravel. Red flags went up regarding the birth mother. However, it wasn't until after Nathan was born that we completely understood what we were facing. God kept it from us until He knew the time was right.

Nathan is almost ten years old now. I cannot explain the miracles that God has wrought in his young life. He is a strong, healthy, vibrant child. It has not been all rosy, I can assure you. We have had intense struggles. But I thank God for keeping our eyes veiled. If He had shown us everything from the beginning, I undoubtedly would have run away in fear. In His mercy, He lifted the veil inches at a time so we could stand firm in obedience.

God was about to do the unthinkable through Peter. He was going to cross cultural and religious lines that would incite intense opposition and misunderstanding. The inclusion of the Gentiles in the exact same manner as the Jews into the kingdom of God was unfathomable to the devout Jew. Even Gentile proselytes into the Jewish religion had to remain in a separate section of the temple. Equality between the two groups was unexplainable. God had to keep Peter in the dark until it would be difficult for Peter to disobey or deny what God was doing.

Does your faith journey feel dark today, friend? Are you trying to move forward but cannot tell where God is headed? Take heart! Remember, when we want God to do something unexplainable, we have to follow Him to places that have yet to be explained to us.

What do you sense the Holy Spirit whispering to your heart today?

WEEK 8 | DAY 5
THE UNEXPLAINABLE HOLY SPIRIT
Please read aloud ACTS 10:47–48

I'm pretty much always sticking my foot in my mouth. The proverb is true—lots of talking leads to foolish speech (Proverbs 10:19). This week someone posted a snarky meme about atheism. I found it funny and reposted it. Much to my surprise, I had several atheists comment on it, arguing their position. *Adamantly*, I might add.

I quickly realized my inadequacy in attempting to defend my faith. One part of me just wanted to remove the post. The other part of me knew that was exactly what these people who commented were hoping I would do. I felt stuck. One of the pastors at our church, an expert apologist, graciously chimed in with a logical, well-formulated response.

The Holy Spirit convicted me of a great deficit. I need to be ready to logically explain my faith. I need to have gracious responses when people attack me.

What does Peter tell us in 1 Peter 3:15?

I wonder if Peter recalled that moment before Cornelius's household when he penned that letter. Here he stood in front of a high-ranking Roman official as he shared the gospel. Remember, Peter was a fisherman. He was uneducated, from a small town in Israel, and way out of his league standing before members of the Roman aristocracy.

Have we taken time to think through how we might present our faith to various audiences?

Whether to Jews or Gentiles, Peter's presentation of salvation to all people was offensive. To the Jews, the inclusion of the Gentiles meant their privileged position of receiving God's favor had been extended to others. And the Gentiles had to accept that God's plan of salvation had been offered through the Jews, whom they viewed as inferior.

How does Paul now describe the relationship of the Jews and the Gentiles as a result of Christ's death and resurrection according to Ephesians 2:11–22?

The dividing wall of hostility refers to the temple. Women, along with Gentiles who had converted to Judaism, were welcomed into the outer court, while only Jewish men were allowed into the inner court. Paul is claiming there is now no distinction.

How does Paul reemphasize this truth in Colossians 3:11?

See Romans 10:12–15.
What does Paul admonish us to do as a result of this oneness among Jew and Gentile?

It is difficult to overcome cultural bias and preconceived notions. Even though Peter willingly went into Cornelius's house, preached the gospel to these Gentiles, witnessed the Holy Spirit being poured out among them, and then baptized them into the family of believers, he still reverted to his previous stance of the necessity of the observance of Judaism.

What happened in Galatians 2:11–16?

Many Jews believed that for the Gentiles to become believers in Jesus as the Jewish Messiah, they needed to not only accept the gospel message but follow the Jewish laws and customs as well. Among other requirements, men had to be circumcised. While Peter acknowledged the inclusion of the Gentiles into God's kingdom, he still had moments of twisting the gift of grace by putting stipulations on Gentile inclusion.

Some of the Jews in this camp insisted that Paul made it too easy for Gentiles to receive salvation. They believed these converts needed to become Jews first. Paul argued that is was not by observing the law that anyone was justified or saved from their sins—it happened solely by faith.

How does Paul explain this concept in Ephesians 2:8–9?

When you and I share the gospel message with others, we need to explain it thoroughly and adequately. We cannot downplay sin, but we cannot shame or condemn either. We need to be mindful of our audience and the preconceived notions they hold.

Acts 17:22–33 is a remarkable passage. Note how Paul customizes the gospel message for the men of Athens.

- He started with familiar concepts.
- He acknowledged their beliefs and then moved forward, explaining how his belief in Christ fit in with their own life experiences.
- He recognized and affirmed that they were men of reason who cared about the truth. He didn't approach them as ignorant fools.

- He didn't ridicule their conclusions.
- He presented the gospel logically and respectfully starting with the knowledge base and beliefs of his audience.

Oh, that we could follow Paul's example when sharing Christ with others! Going back to 1 Peter 3:15–16, may this be our goal whenever we are asked to give the reason for the hope that is in us: "Always be prepared to give an answer to everyone who asks you to give the reason for the hope that you have. But do this with gentleness and respect, keeping a clear conscience, so that those who speak maliciously against your good behavior in Christ may be ashamed of their slander" (NIV).

The elements of the gospel must be maintained, but the analogies and stories that bring those elements to life should be fitted to our audience.

A year or so ago my friend Jennifer asked me to come speak at her home. She invited her friends and neighbors for appetizers and introduced me to them. I asked the women to share how each knew Jennifer, and the answers varied greatly. One woman was clearly uncomfortable with my many references to God as I shared stories about the importance of women having relationships with other women. I was honestly afraid she might get up and leave. When it came time for me to clearly present the gospel, the Lord prompted me to share how inadequate and afraid I felt as a young mom. I wanted to do everything perfectly while raising our new daughter. A brand-new mom herself, I saw this woman's heart soften. Her body relaxed and she leaned in, listening intently to what I was saying. I explained how salvation related to my fears of not being able to do everything perfectly. We need Jesus to cover us where we don't measure up. This resonated with her.

At the end of the night, I raffled off a couple of my books. When I drew her name, I quickly followed with, "No one *has* to take one if they don't want it. I won't be offended, I promise. Bible studies aren't for everyone!" To which she quickly replied, "Oh my, I was hoping you would call my name!" The Holy Spirit had pierced her heart. She began to thirst to understand God more deeply. The Holy

Spirit led me to speak to her as one mother to another.

Let's think about some of the demographics of our audiences. How could you customize your presentation of the gospel to the following groups:

A stay-at-home mom by using a family analogy:

An ambitious student by using a professor/student analogy:

A person suffering from a chronic condition by using a physician/healing analogy:

An agnostic who may believe God exists but that He is distant or apathetic by using a friendship/family analogy:

We won't always have all the answers. We won't ever be so prepared that some-one won't stump us with a question we cannot immediately answer. But part of presenting the gospel with gentleness and respect comes from validating the person. Sometimes we will be attacked. Sometimes we will even be ridiculed. But sometimes the Holy Spirit will come and pierce through a heart of stone with the reality of Christ. And when He does, it's pretty unexplainable.

Make a list of people in your circle of influence. Circle one name with whom you will share the gospel this week. Ask someone to hold you accountable. Then pray for the Holy Spirit to work.

unexplainable discipleship

SOME QUESTIONS

Please read aloud ACTS 11:1–17

It's important we understand how incredulous it was for the Holy Spirit to be poured out on the Gentiles. So much so, that Luke records the entire episode a second time in the book of Acts, this time told firsthand by Peter. When we remember that "books" in Luke's day were written on large, expensive pieces of parchment, we begin to understand the importance of this event at Cornelius's home! Since Luke may have been a Gentile himself, as was Theophilus, it makes sense that Gentile inclusion would be dear to his heart. In both accounts, Luke emphasizes the initiation and work of God in the process.

When we are talking about "Gentiles," we are talking about a current political enemy, imposing laws and taxes contrary to Jewish beliefs and in direct opposition to their worship of Yahweh. The Jewish people felt oppressed by the Romans. Their relationship was not merely a difference of opinion or values—the Romans *subjugated* the Jews. We have to understand this contextually, though it is difficult in our Western mindset to do so.

How did the Jewish believers in Jerusalem respond to Peter's news in Acts 11:1–3?

In first-century Israel, people shared meals much differently than we do today. A communal dish would be set in the middle of the table from which everyone ate, and pieces of bread were torn off and dipped into the common bowl. Double dipping was definitely allowed! The one piece of meat would be touched by everyone at the table.

Eating was a much more intimate experience than it is in our Western society, where we use individual plates and utensils. Back then, people could not eat together without touching one another and touching the same items. Imagine going out to dinner with a group of coworkers, passing around a drumstick, and having everyone take a bite. Partaking of a meal together meant much more than just sitting across the table from someone. This helps us understand why Jews were forbidden to eat with Gentiles.

It appears that Peter did not return to Jerusalem immediately after his encounter at Cornelius's house. He continued traveling, ministering to various groups of saints throughout Judea and Samaria. News of the event had reached Jerusalem, however, and when Peter returned the believers demanded an explanation from him.

Read Acts 11:8–9.
How does Peter's retelling of his vision demonstrate that it took awhile for him to get the message?

What was God's response to Peter's rebuttal?

What had Jesus previously said to Peter when Peter argued with Him in Matthew 16:21–23?

What else did Jesus say to him in John 13:6–8?

It is generally not a good idea to argue with God! In all three instances, Peter responded with an emotional reaction, failing to understand what God was doing. But oh, the patience of Jesus! It has been six or seven years since Jesus ascended, commanding them to take the gospel message to the world. Until Peter goes to Cornelius's home, he had yet to share the gospel with a single Gentile! He knew what Jesus had told him, he heard the words that Jesus had spoken, but he failed to understand. It took incredible, divine intervention through dovetailed visions to get Peter to realize what he was to do.

Have you ever had an experience in your life when God demonstrated His unlimited patience toward you? Share it with your group.

See Acts 11:11–12.
So here we have God speaking to Peter in a vision. Meanwhile, what does the Holy Spirit do in this scene?

Who went with Peter to Caesarea?

The group of believers sent on this mission totaled seven. The number seven in Jewish thought represented completeness or finality. From the Gentile perspective, it took seven seals under Roman law to authenticate a document. To any of Luke's readers, Jew or Gentile, the inclusion of seven witnesses verifying the work of the Holy Spirit in the Gentiles' lives held significance.

Peter adds an additional detail in the retelling of his experience that Luke left out the first time. Compare Acts 10:30–33 with Acts 11:13–14. Record what additional information Cornelius adds about Peter's message.

Read Acts 11:13–15. How does Peter describe the messenger in Cornelius's vision?

How does Peter describe the work of the Holy Spirit?

What had Peter declared when the Holy Spirit had been poured out in the beginning, back in Acts 2:38–39?

Under the divine inspiration of the Holy Spirit at Pentecost, Peter spoke that those who were "far off," meaning those who were not children of Israel, would receive the Holy Spirit if they called on the name of Jesus. Here we are several years later, but Peter has apparently forgotten all about this. Suddenly, the Holy Spirit illuminates the Word to him.

See Acts 11:16–17.
What did Peter "remember"?

Notice Peter did not attempt to justify his behavior solely based on a vision. He explained his actions based on John the Baptist's prophecy to them back in Mark 1:8. When we sense God trying to get our attention through multiple means, we best pay attention!

Have you ever had an experience where you felt like God was trying to get your attention through His written Word, the spoken word, and circumstantial intervention all at the same time? Describe the circumstance and what you felt God was trying to teach you in the process.

Ironically, we heard this same question posed in regard to the gospel message earlier in Acts. Who suggested they may be fighting against God in Acts 5:34–39 and to which group was he referring?

We see from Peter's explanation that he is equally shocked by the dispensation of the Holy Spirit among the Gentiles as his Jerusalem brothers. The unification between these two groups of people was truly unexplainable apart from the power of the Holy Spirit allowing them to cross racial, ethnic, cultural, and religious boundaries. In Jesus' kingdom there is no male, female, race, ethnicity, or cultural preference. We are all simply children of God.

Of course, just as the enemy tried to create division among the Hellenistic Jews and the Palestinian Jews back in Acts 6, we will see him start to create havoc among the Jews and the Gentiles. Whenever there is distinction and division among God's church, we know the enemy is at work.

What are some ways you see the enemy creating division in the church today?

What are some practical ways to bring about greater unity within the church?

We may choose to stand in our corners and only stick with those people and customs we find most comfortable. But in the process, we just may find ourselves fighting against God.

EXPERIENCE AND THE WORD

Please read aloud ACTS 11:16–20

Peter recounted to his Jewish brothers in Jerusalem several proofs that God clearly intended the inclusion of the Gentiles into the church. First, he emphasized the message of the visions both he and Cornelius received. Then he recounted the commandment of Jesus to baptize the Gentiles as well as the Jewish people. He insisted the Holy Spirit sent him to Cornelius's house and that a complete number of Jewish brethren, namely seven, witnessed the Holy Spirit's arrival just as it had come upon them at Pentecost. I think we can say that God made His wishes abundantly clear!

What was the reaction of the Jewish believers? Write Acts 11:18 here:

Now, this truly is one of my favorite verses in the Bible. These Jewish men praised God for including the Gentiles. They did not begrudgingly concede to their admittance into the kingdom. They did not *tolerate* their reception of the Holy Spirit; instead, they *praised God!* Think of the humility required for them to respond as such. Imagine being victimized by someone who demoralized you, robbed you, and treated you with contempt. Then later you heard the person had become a believer. Would you praise God, or would you be angry because now you might wonder if he would be repaid for all of the evil he had done to you? I'll confess— that would be tough for me!

The Jewish believers appeared to fully understand the depths of God's forgiveness. They were grateful for their salvation and humble in heart. They knew they were no more worthy of the grace given to them than any Gentile. This, my friends, depicts the attitude of Christ.

What does Philippians 2:6–8 tell us of Christ's humility?

Read Acts 11:19–21.
While Peter was sharing the gospel in Caesarea at Cornelius's house, who else was sharing the gospel and where?

To whom were they specifically sharing it?

Now, none of these cities were within the boundaries of Israel, so Luke is emphasizing that the gospel is spreading farther and farther. However, the Jewish believers at large still misunderstood the mission of going to the Gentiles. There are always those few followers of Jesus, however, who are willing to move boldly ahead.

What was happening in Antioch?

The Jewish believers in verse 19 probably were Palestinian Jews. They fled due to persecution, but they had not been previously immersed in Greek culture. Sheltered in the highly Jewish population of Palestine, they immediately sought out their Jewish brethren who lived in the cities to which they had fled. The Jewish believers in Acts 11:20 were not Palestinian Jews however.

Where does Luke tell us these Jews were from?

Cyprus is an island off the coast of Syria in the Mediterranean Sea, with a long-standing Greek influence. Cyrene was a port on the northern tip of Africa. Jews from these cities grew up among Gentiles, similar to Saul's upbringing in Tarsus, and would have been fluent in Greek. These men went to the Greeks and shared the gospel.

How can you see your own cultural or ethnic background equipping you to share the gospel to certain people groups?

How can you see your life experiences working or living in different places equipping you to share the gospel?

Can you think of an example when someone was willing to take the gospel to an unreached people group?

What did the Holy Spirit do as a result of their willingness to go to the Greeks with the gospel? See verse 21.

The Holy Spirit burst on the scene at Pentecost followed by changed disciples and miraculous signs and wonders. Within the first year, Philip went to Samaria and revival occurred. Now we are seven to eight years into church history, and after an initial explosion of the Holy Spirit and vast numbers of Jewish people coming to Christ, the growth of the church seems to have slowed. We are not told of any more dynamic sermons with thousands accepting the message. Peter's miracles seem to have lessened. The church seems to have begun to function in a predictable rhythm.

Then, suddenly, the Holy Spirit falls on Cornelius's family. Shortly thereafter, the Holy Spirit is on the move again. More and more Gentiles are coming to faith in Christ. Have you heard the admonition, "Find out where the Spirit is working and then go there"?

Where do you see the Spirit working today?

When was the last time you sensed the Holy Spirit moving and working in a particular group of people or venue?

Sometimes we do not sense His movement as much as we would like to. What could be some reasons for this?

I don't know about you, but I would love to see the Holy Spirit spark revival in my church. I would love to see racial reconciliation happen in unexplainable ways within my community. I would be thrilled to see people I love come to faith in Christ Jesus. I think our first step is recognizing our need for the Holy Spirit. The perfectly planned event won't do it. The high-profile speaker won't guarantee it. Only the Spirit of God can draw people's hearts.

We need to ask the Holy Spirit to examine our own hearts to see if there is something we are doing to grieve Him. If He brings something to mind, then we need to repent and ask for grace to obey. Maybe then He'll be ready to do the unexplainable among us!

If you could ask the Holy Spirit to come and do something unexplainable among you, what would it be and why?

Spend some time in prayer today allowing the Spirit to speak to you in the quietness of your heart. Record what He reveals to you below:

THE RIGHT MAN FOR THE JOB

Please read aloud ACTS 11:21–30

Yesterday we met some more unnamed heroes of our faith. Jews from Cyprus and Cyrene took the message of Christ to the Gentiles. God blessed their faithfulness, and many who heard their message turned to the Lord. These were faithful followers who recognized the commands of God and followed through in obedience even though it would create opposition from their fellow brethren. Some Jewish believers would not understand what they were doing or why they were doing it.

We must emphasize the difference between these Gentiles and the members of Cornelius's household. We are told in Acts that Cornelius feared God. This most likely meant that he recognized the wisdom and righteousness of observing God's law and worshiping only Yahweh but was probably not circumcised, and therefore not considered a true proselyte to Judaism.

But the Gentiles in Antioch did not fear God. They were most likely steeped in pagan worship. At this time, Antioch was the third largest city in the Roman Empire, after Rome and Alexandria. Since it was the capital city of the Syrian portion of the empire, Romans lived there along with Jews and Greeks. It was a wealthy, cosmopolitan, multicultural gathering place. The city housed the center of the cult of Apollo, known for gross sexual immorality. This gives us an idea as to the nature of the previous religious activities of some of these new converts.

Read Acts 11:22–25.
Why did the Jewish church in Jerusalem believe they needed to check out the Antioch revival?

What did Barnabas notice when he arrived, and how did he feel about it?

How did Barnabas, the Son of Encouragement, encourage these new believers?

Find three characteristics attributed to Barnabas in this passage.

What resulted from Barnabas's time in Antioch?

Why did Barnabas leave Antioch?

Barnabas may have known these unnamed Jews from Cyprus who were spreading the gospel in Antioch. After all, he was originally from Cyprus. Barnabas again saves the day. Not an apostle or a deacon, he was yet indispensable in times of confusion. Barnabas seems to be the guy who is willing to follow the Holy Spirit wherever He may lead. It was Barnabas who welcomed Paul. Now Barnabas is called into a potentially disturbing situation. Who are these men taking the gospel to the pagan Gentiles who have nothing to do with Judaism?

Oh, to be a Barnabas! One who is able to correct gently, initiate reconciliation, encourage the confused, and who brings peace to troubling situations! Think of the trust the apostles placed in him. None of the apostles accompanied Barnabas to Antioch. Whatever Barnabas reported to them, they would believe and accept.

Of all Barnabas's qualities, which ones do you most admire?

How might Barnabas have developed into a man so willing to follow the leading of the Spirit?

Upon his arrival, even more Gentiles are brought to faith in Christ (Acts 11:24)! You would think that in the middle of all this excitement, Barnabas would settle down in Antioch, anticipating what the Holy Spirit might do next. But Barnabas doesn't stay; he goes to Tarsus and gets Paul. Think about his decision to do this. Last time Barnabas had seen Paul, he had escorted him to board a ship to head back to his hometown. Several years have now passed. Perhaps Barnabas remembered Paul's account of how Jesus had commissioned him to take the gospel to the Gentiles.

Think of Barnabas's humility! The Spirit is being poured out. A great number of Gentiles are coming to Christ, and Barnabas brings in Paul. He could have easily headed up this group of new believers himself, but instead he honestly assesses the circumstances and his abilities and concludes, "I know just the right person to bring into this situation to establish these young believers: Paul!" It takes a lot of humility to share the spotlight with someone else when it's been shining on you with incredible brightness. It also took incredible reconciliatory and peace-making skills. These unnamed believers who started this revival in Antioch could have resented Barnabas's and then Paul's arrival. Who were they to come into town and take over the work that God had allowed them to start?

I think Barnabas's admonition to these young believers gives us a glimpse into why Barnabas was able to be so humble. Finish Acts 11:23 below:

"When he came and saw the grace of God, he exhorted [encouraged] them _____

_____

_____."

Barnabas had no personal agenda. His only aim was to remain true to the Lord, steadfast in purpose. He did this in both mind and heart. We can intellectually assent to a philosophy or idea, but until we purpose in our heart to live wholeheartedly in the truth of it, we may waver in our resolve depending on circumstances. Barnabas was continually led by the Spirit, because he had committed in his heart to follow the Spirit no matter the cost. I think these unnamed evangelists recognized the purity of Barnabas's heart, allowing them to welcome both he and Paul into the work that God had started through them.

Have you ever experienced someone arriving to take over something you started? If so, did you experience purity in your heart or resentment at feeling shoved aside?

How would you describe your own faith: does it begin and end with an intellectual assent? or is it lived out by the resolve of your heart and mind? Write out a resolution below to follow the Holy Spirit's leading. Include people, circumstances, or things that you feel prompted to hand over to the Lord:

Barnabas was willing to follow the Holy Spirit to people and places that the Jewish believers in Jerusalem preferred to avoid. As a result, he witnessed the Spirit do the unexplainable. As much as we don't want to admit it, I believe we often miss the Holy Spirit's work because we hesitate to be uncomfortable. Or we are distracted by our own agenda. We love Jesus but we are not true to Him with *all* of our heart. We have other affections that tug at our heartstrings: goals, ambitions, relationships, desires, comforts, pleasures. These aren't necessarily sinful pursuits, they can just keep us from chasing after the Spirit. They keep us from experiencing the unexplainable in our lives.

THE IMPORTANCE OF DISCIPLESHIP

Please read aloud ACTS 11:25–26

I find two types of Christians to be incredibly inspiring. The first have a God-given vision for ministry on their heart to meet a specific need or to reach a specific group of people. Their soul becomes filled with such yearning to see the idea come to fruition, they will spend countless hours and resources to make it happen. They become relentless in their obedience to God in fulfilling what He has laid on their heart. They press on in joy, assured that God is with them guiding their steps.

The second are those who are so kingdom focused that they are less concerned with where they fit in God's kingdom plans and instead are constantly looking for ways to help others find their place within the body. Weaving people with different giftedness together, they connect the dots, bringing just the right groups of people together to help these visionaries bring their plans to fruition. Never concerned with their own role within the work, they search the hearts and passions of those around them, encouraging them to step out in service. It takes true selflessness to be devoted to God's plans or His people over our own agenda.

I think Barnabas was both. He had a vision for these new believers to be established in Antioch, equipped with solid teaching to fully understand Jesus. He realized the Holy Spirit was on the move reaching people who knew nothing of the lifestyle of Judaism. These young believers needed intense discipleship because their faith in Jesus necessitated a radical shift in their current lifestyle. Unlike the Jews who were already moral, religious, and devout in their worship of Yahweh, these Antioch believers had been immoral, corrupt, and steeped in pagan worship. This was going to be tough, and they would need an incredibly strong leader to keep them on the right path.

Paul of Tarsus was just the man! Luke does not inform us what Paul had been doing for the last several years. Of what we can be sure, God was preparing Paul for the ministry He had for him.

For Deeper Discoveries on examples of people God tucked away in preparation, visit ericawiggenhorn.com.

Once Barnabas found Paul in Tarsus, what did they do (Acts 11:26)?

What verb describes the predominant action of Barnabas and Paul during this time?

What name was given to this group of believers?

This is the first time Luke describes the work of instructing or teaching. Up to this point, the gospel message was shared through preaching or explaining. Something different is happening here. These new believers required another level of instruction. Barnabas recognized this need and was as equally committed to establishing them in their faith as he was to evangelizing them.

Many churches today emphasize preaching the gospel. Their services are purposely planned to present Jesus to people who may never have heard of Him before or who have limited knowledge of the tenets of the faith. These churches serve a mighty purpose in delivering the gospel to a world who needs to hear it.

If you attend a church with this approach, however, it is important for you to receive additional instruction in order to grow in your knowledge and faith; your church may offer classes or small study groups. If your only exposure to discipleship is a repetition of the basics of the salvation message over and over again every Sunday, without added depth of biblical teaching, it will prove difficult to grow in your faith and understanding of what it means to follow Jesus. You will begin to get the idea that now that you have been "saved," you have it all figured out and there is nothing more to learn. The Jewish believers understood that following Jesus altered their entire identity and consumed their existence. These Gentile believers needed to be taught the same.

What did Paul say in Galatians 2:19–20?

What else did Paul say about our life in Colossians 3:3?

Even the most adept pastor will tell you that additional teaching is beneficial. Do we long to know the Scriptures inside and out?

Would you describe your church services as seeker-focused, teaching-focused, or a combination?

How does your church evangelize, i.e., present the basics of the gospel, and also offer opportunities for believers to grow in biblical knowledge and the Christian walk?

Once after a speaking engagement, someone come up to me and said, "You actually taught me something new from the Bible. I know my Bible pretty well and it is rare that someone teaches me something I don't already know." I commented, "You must be committed to studying your Bible then!" "Well yes," she replied, leafing through one of my Bible study books, "and I'd like to do one of your studies with the women I lead, but I just can't imagine them committing to reading a few pages a day to learn the Bible. This would take entirely too much time!"

I will not lie to you. I was disappointed. This woman herself was versed in the Word. Her knowledge of the Scriptures resulted in her church leadership entrusting her with teaching other women. Yet she did not think the women she led would commit to a daily time of studying the Bible more deeply. We have become a culture committed to bite-sized instruction. Carving out twenty, thirty, or forty minutes a day to study the Scripture sounds like an eternity.

Why do you suppose so few people are willing to study the Bible daily?

What would your response have been to the Bible study leader with whom I spoke?

What does this portion of Scripture teach us about the importance of becoming avid students of the Word of God?

These young believers at Antioch learned from both Barnabas and Paul. These guys were polar opposites! While some probably loved Paul's intensity, others may have found him annoying. Barnabas's gracious manner attracted many, but those living in rebellion may not have taken him seriously. Paul could be a bit more intimidating in his command to obey. God brought both men together to strike the perfect balance to equip and establish the church.

No doubt they learned from one another as much as they taught together. Paul learned to be more gracious and encouraging, while Barnabas became more forthright and courageous. Their bents in personality sharpened one another, preparing both of them for greater service elsewhere. Barnabas would be called to mentor a young man who continued to rebel against God's call on his life. He needed to learn how to speak the truth firmly like Paul in order to help shape and equip the timid John Mark, who we will get to know more fully in the last week of our study. Both Paul and Barnabas were equally valuable to each other.

Have you ever served alongside someone of a much different personality than yours? What did God teach you during your time together?

Would you say that you are more like Paul or Barnabas? How so?

What are some areas in which you would like to grow, enabling you to serve the body with greater excellence?

How committed are you to your own growth in the knowledge of the Scriptures— as well as dealing with people—to become more fully equipped to serve?

It took years of preparation for Paul to be ready to come and learn from Barnabas. Paul knew the Scriptures. He could explain them perfectly. Where he needed to grow was in humility of heart and graciousness. God paired him up with the perfect teacher. Sometimes we fail to see how God may be using the people around us to prepare us for an unexplainable adventure!

Take a mental survey of your relationships. Who do you suppose God may be using in your life to help shape and equip you?

Who might God be asking you to help shape and equip?

Just like with Paul and Barnabas, any relationship is a two-way street. Someone has a vision given by God. Maybe it's you. Or maybe you are the person to come alongside the visionary and help fulfill the goal. Or maybe you are the person meant to see the potential in others to aid in its fulfillment. Either way, we must know the Scriptures if we are going to stay true to Christ's mission. And we must work together if we're going to see God do something unexplainable!

WEEK 9 | DAY 5
THE GLOBAL CHURCH
Please read aloud ACTS 11:27–30

In Jewish heritage, a name holds great significance. A person's name not only indicates their purpose but also determines their destiny. This is why there are so many accounts of God giving people specific names throughout the Bible. It also helps us understand why God repeatedly gave different names to Himself throughout Israel's history. It revealed His purpose and His future plans.

For this reason, I find it interesting that the "church" was not named until the inclusion of the Gentile believers at Antioch. The Holy Spirit's ultimate purpose was fulfilled when He was poured out on all people, not limited to Jews. The destiny of Christ's message was to spread to every nation, tribe, and tongue. Once this began to happen, the church was officially named. And what was the name they were given? Christians.

We see the solidarity between the Gentile and Jewish church. Not only did the Jerusalem church send Barnabas, they also sent additional visitors.

Read Acts 11:27–30.
Who did the Jerusalem church send to Antioch?

What did Agabus predict?

We have yet to hear of the Samaritan and Judean believers caring for one another, but here we are told how the Gentile church will provide for their Jewish brethren in Judea. Claudius began to reign as emperor in AD 41 and continued until AD 54. This does not tell us exactly when Agabus prophesied about the famine, but the structure of Luke's writing intimates that Claudius had not yet begun to reign when the prophecy occurred. If that is so, then the church as a whole is somewhere between eight to ten years old, placing Jesus's death and resurrection around AD 30 or 33.

Remember, Antioch was a wealthy Roman city, boasting a seat of government, and many of these Gentile believers were likely also well-off. By this time, we know there were groups of believers spread throughout Judea, Samaria, and the northern tip of Africa. The church had become global.

In New Testament times, people relied on letters, personal visits, or word of mouth to disseminate news. Today we have many more resources at our disposal.

How regularly do you hear about what is happening in the global church?

How can we be informed about the church around the world?

Why should we intentionally educate ourselves about what God is doing throughout the world?

How could hearing stories about what is happening in other parts of the world encourage us? convict us?

Is there a particular part of the world to which you feel drawn? Have you ever thought of taking a mission trip there or visiting? (If you do, *Helping without Hurting in Short-Term Missions* by Steve Corbett and Brian Fikkert is a great resource. Taking a mission trip requires preparation and knowledge in order to truly be of service to Christians in another culture.)

I love to meet Christians from other parts of the United States and the world. It is so encouraging to hear what God is doing in their midst. When we step outside of our usual environment, we are awakened that God is on the move everywhere! It's refreshing to experience the bond of another believer who, only five minutes prior, was a complete stranger. It reminds me that I am part of a kingdom so much bigger than myself and all that is familiar to me. It makes me excited for heaven!

Have you ever randomly met another Christian and instantly felt connected to them?

How did God use that experience to encourage or inspire you?

On the flip side, researchers and psychologists have determined a new condition called "compassion fatigue." It comes from being repeatedly presented with so many needs that a person can no longer respond with adequate or appropriate emotion. In America, where we live in excess and exercise our faith freely, could it be we have distanced ourselves from the global church because we do not want to be confronted with their needs? The people of Antioch lived in a thriving, beautiful city. The life of a Judean farmer struggling to barely feed his family was completely foreign to them. If the prophet had not come to this church, they would have remained completely unaware of the need.

When and where would you say you have experienced compassion fatigue?

How can we balance being presented with so many needs in the world and responding appropriately?

How do you decide to which needs you will respond with your own time and/or resources?

When Luke tells us each disciple at Antioch gave "according to his ability" what do you think he means—sacrificially? or out of their excess?

How does our heart for the global church make us unexplainable in the eyes of the world?

None of us need to be prophets to know the world is full of needs. We don't have to study history very long to know the needs are not going away. Part of becoming like Christ is to fellowship with Him in His sufferings—to experience His empathy for those who are in want or persecution. One day we will all reign together with Him and all our crying and pain will end. For now, we all have something to do—our local church and the global church. Let's get busy, shall we?

a journey
toward an
unexplainable
life

MORE MARTYRDOM

Please read aloud ACTS 12:1–3

We have been on quite the journey together these last nine weeks, haven't we, friend? It is hard to believe we have covered the first decade of church history . . . and so much has happened! From Jesus' ascension to the outpouring of the Holy Spirit at Pentecost, miraculous signs and wonders performed by the apostles, Philip's incredible evangelistic exploits to the Samaritans and the Ethiopian eunuch, all climaxing with the outpouring of the Holy Spirit on Cornelius's household and the Gentiles in Antioch. So many different people, spread across continents, all working together by the power of the Holy Spirit to further the kingdom. Unexplainable!

As readily as we recount His incredible deeds through the apostles and deacons, we must also remember the incredible work of the Holy Spirit in and through the lay believers. Men like Ananias, Simon, and Barnabas, women like Tabitha, and the unnamed heroes who spread the gospel in Antioch all stir in us our own call within the kingdom. Clearly the message of Acts is the intricacy in which the Holy Spirit weaves every member of Christ's church together to accomplish His mission. Every believer is indispensable!

This first decade further demonstrates the promise that each of our individual journeys toward an unexplainable life is a process within God's sovereign control. The Holy Spirit transforms our hearts and lives and spreads the gospel. The church individually and collectively will continue to survive despite any opposition that may come against it. Attacks within and without could not stop the spread of the gospel. As we begin our last week together, we find church persecution escalating, all the while being reminded that God continues to work in the hearts of His people, perpetuating the good news from generation to generation. The church is unstoppable!

Read Acts 12:1–3.

What was King Herod doing in Jerusalem?

What happened to James?

How did the Jewish people in Jerusalem respond, and how did their response spur on Herod?

During what Jewish holy day was this all transpiring?

We read of King Herod several times throughout the New Testament, so let's talk about him for a bit. The King Herod mentioned here by Luke is Herod Agrippa I, the grandson of King Herod the Great, who ordered the death of Hebrew boys under the age of two (Matthew 2:16), causing Mary and Joseph to flee to Egypt after Jesus was born. He is also the nephew of Herod Antipas who ordered John the Baptist to be beheaded after John denounced Antipas for marrying his half-brother's wife. King Herod in Acts surely knew of Jesus and was somewhat familiar with His teachings. The fact that we are now twenty to thirty years past Jesus' death and resurrection troubled him. The Jesus followers were not going away. In fact, their numbers were growing. And now these Jewish men were converting Gentiles into their movement. Most troubling indeed.

So Herod decided to take action. Not being entirely certain how his actions might be perceived, Herod calculated his course strategically. The first two verses in Acts 12 tell us that he "laid violent hands on some who belonged to the church" and that "he killed James the brother of John with the sword." When he saw that this pleased the Jews, he arrested Peter. In this way, if the Jews disliked his course of action, perhaps they would voice their displeasure for a while, but would soon lose interest and move on to other issues. Peter and John were widely known for their wonderful miracles. Killing them might create havoc among the people. Ultimately, Herod sought to destroy the leadership of the church in order to weaken it.

Herein presents another tactic of the enemy against the church: the targeting of the leadership. Christians fall into sin and make mistakes daily, but when a leader in the Christian community falls prey to temptation, the media pounces. We ought to be diligent in praying for our pastors and other high-profile Christians, asking God to deliver them from temptation.

How often do we pray for our pastors and their protection? Why might the enemy place greater efforts on destroying the testimony of a pastor or other high-profile Christian?

Herod strategically chose this time of year to take such action as executing James. During the Feast of Unleavened Bread, or the Passover, we know that Jews migrated to Jerusalem from all over the known world. Many would remain within Jerusalem for the fifty days between Passover and Pentecost. Herod sought to capitalize on this Jewish influx, thereby sending a message to Christians worldwide: your movement is considered a form of political insurrection and you shall be punished! Remember, most Jewish Christians still followed Jewish law at this point in church history, so Christian Jews flooded into Jerusalem during these feasts also.

On the flip side, he courted his Roman leaders. We already know that instigations of riots and movements were common among the Jews during these holy days. Gamaliel spelled out some examples for us back in Acts 5. Herod desired to show the empire that he was able to keep his territory under peaceful control during historically volatile seasons. While he appeared to be siding with the Jews in maintaining the supremacy of their worship and their law, his efforts were ultimately self-serving.

During Jewish holy days, courts were not in session. Herod's plan was to send his message at the beginning of the feast, so word would spread among the Jews throughout the week. Once the Holy Week concluded, Herod planned additional attacks on the church, especially once he realized that in doing so, he won the approval of the Jews. While the gospel is spreading, new opposition arises.

As we'll see tomorrow, though James the brother of John has been killed, the Lord spares Peter in these attacks against the church. It is hard to understand why God did not intervene in both men's lives identically. Whatever God purposed James to do in His kingdom, he faithfully completed. Peter still had other purposes to fulfill: one of them being to write his epistles and another to give John Mark a firsthand account of all that Jesus said and did for the construction of his gospel. We cannot know when God will call any of us home, but what we can claim is that God will protect His children while they are here, allowing them to carry out the purpose for which He created them. In other words, you and I each have a destiny to fulfill in God's kingdom plans.

How does that last sentence make you feel? How intentional are you in discovering what your purpose may be?

Read Ephesians 2:10 and write the verse here:

What are some practical ways to intentionally pursue the "good works, which God prepared beforehand" for us to do as described in Ephesians 2?

The second thing we need to remember is that death was not necessarily considered a tragedy to these early Christians. Now the process of death—that is another story, but to die for the sake of Christ was a deep honor.

We can surmise that James would have echoed the words Paul penned some years later: "For to me to live is Christ, and to die is gain" (Philippians 1:21). He welcomed reunification with Jesus when his time came. In the meantime, you and I have a purpose to fulfill. And those in leadership hold a purpose with the potential to impact many for the kingdom of God or the kingdom of darkness. Regardless of what role we have, we are all called to pray—fervently.

Spend some time today praying for your pastor and those in church leadership. Pray also for high-profile Christians you know: musicians, teachers, missionaries, speakers, and anyone else the Lord may bring to mind.

See Deeper Discoveries at ericawiggenhorn.com to learn more about the role of the apostles according to Jesus.

PETER IMPRISONED

Please read aloud ACTS 12:3–12

James beheaded and Peter imprisoned: a difficult beginning to the week of Passover. Of Jesus' three most intimate disciples, Peter, James, and John, only one remains free: John, James's brother. He is presumably grieving the loss of his brother while determining whether to flee Jerusalem or stay to lead the church. No doubt the believers were terrified. This passage of Acts informs us that other believers were also arrested along with James and Peter. Imagine discovering that your pastor and several of your church's staff members had been arrested. Word on the street was that anyone affiliated with them may suffer the same end. What do you do?

See Acts 12:3–5.
What did Herod intend to do with Peter?

How did the believers respond?

Don't you love that? In the midst of his imprisonment, the church supported Peter through "earnest prayer."

Oh, that our churches would gather in prayer in a time of crisis! May we find ourselves inviting other believers over to pray about an urgent need or specific issue, instead of turning to social media to vent our concerns. Prayer is the invitation for God's intervention. Herein lies the protocol for the impossible to be done: prayer. May we gather together on our knees asking the Holy Spirit to do the unexplainable!

Read Acts 12:6–12.
While Peter is in prison, describe his state of mind as implied in verse 6.

I love that—Peter is snoring away the night before his execution! I believe the church was praying for Peter to have peace and courage. I don't think the believers were praying for Peter to be miraculously delivered from prison; they probably considered him a dead man. Nevertheless, for seven solid days the church earnestly prayed for him. No public trials were performed during this Jewish Holy Week. I've often wondered why God kept Peter imprisoned for the full seven days before miraculously delivering him. Then something occurred to me.

Maybe it was like this: news of Peter's impending trial would spread throughout the city of Jerusalem during this Holy Week. Many Jews would plan on watching it. It would be the weekly entertainment. Knowing exactly when it would take place, many would structure their Holy Week activities enabling them to attend. And when Peter was called to appear, what wonderful miracle would have to be explained? Peter had escaped! Guarded by four Roman soldiers and chained to two of them, somehow Peter had gotten away. How could this be? God was giving the Jewish people another opportunity to witness His favor on Christians and turn their hearts toward His Son.

The story of Peter's escape would be ten times more intriguing than his trial. This news would spread even faster—causing Jews to speculate if and how and why God may have intervened on Peter's behalf. What a good lesson for us when God seems to be slow to intervene in our situations! It may be that we have to wait and endure our trial longer than we would prefer in order for God to use our trial to get someone else's attention!

Describe a time when you were waiting on God to answer a prayer and it seemed like He wasn't listening.

How does Peter's waiting in prison for seven days give you hope that God's seeming failure to act has a deeper purpose of which you may be unaware?

What happened while Peter was sleeping?

What did the angel tell Peter to do, and what was his reaction?

How did Peter and the angel pass through the iron gate?

Once they had left the prison, what did the angel do?

What did Peter suddenly realize?

Where did Peter go next?

I'm amused by the angel telling Peter to get dressed. Wouldn't you want to escape from prison in a hurry, not take the time to put on your clothes? Oh, the irrelevancy of time to God! While the church is fervently praying, God keeps Peter imprisoned for seven long days. When He finally does intervene, Peter is told to carefully dress himself before exiting the prison gate. We are always in such a hurry, aren't we? We live in such a manner that we believe our clock holds more power than our God!

In what ways do you feel pressed for time?

In what ways do you feel time dictates your life: your mood, attitude, decision making, or overall outlook on things?

Why do you suppose the angel made Peter get fully dressed before leading him out of the prison?

While Herod no doubt spent Holy Week thinking with delight about his cleverly concocted schemes, God in His sovereign wisdom held at bay his plans to thwart them. While the church may have been pessimistic that Peter would ever return to them, God knew exactly what He was doing. It is hard to wrap our minds around why God allows certain evil to appear to go unchecked when He holds the power to stop it immediately. Jesus shed some light on this while here on earth.

How did Jesus explain the continuance of evil on the earth in Matthew 13:24–30?

Jesus' kingdom will continue to go forth no matter how many angles of opposition the enemy may throw at it, and the Lord will deal with all things, including evil, at the proper time. We can rest in the fact that time is in His hands. He is never in a hurry and never taken by surprise at any evil that befalls us. He can choose to deliver us from evil or He can deliver us to Himself through death. Either way we are delivered. That is our blessed hope! Either way our purpose is fulfilled, so we spend our days in confidence, trusting that God's plans are unfolding exactly as He has ordained. After all, hope in the midst of evil is always unexplainable to the world.

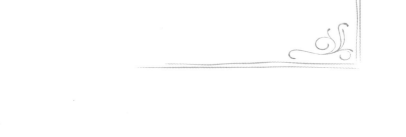

WEEK 10 DAY 3

PRAYER AND FAITH—NOW I KNOW WITHOUT A DOUBT!

Please read aloud ACTS 12:11–23

The night before Peter's scheduled trial and impending execution, an angel miraculously delivers him. Chains fall, iron doors open, and the angel leads Peter out into the city. What a beautiful picture of our own deliverance we are given—unexplainable freedom through Christ's death and resurrection. Remember in verse 9 that Peter didn't know the rescue was actually happening, he thought it was just a vision. But in verse 11 we're told that Peter realized it was really happening! Let's look at Peter's reaction after he realized it wasn't a dream:

"Now I _____

_____."

Are there areas of your life where you'd like to believe for certain that God is working, but you have your doubts?

How would you fill in or hope to fill in the following sentence:

Now I know without a doubt/Now I am certain/sure _____

_____

Maybe through the whole process Peter doubted what was happening to him. He counted it as a dream or a vision but not reality. It wasn't until the event had passed and he could look back on it in its entirety that he fully believed God.

Can you think of a time in your life when you doubted God was working but looking back now you can see that indeed He was? Describe it below:

After Peter's miraculous escape, he first heads to the home of the mother of John Mark, where many believers had gathered praying for Peter. The house must have been fairly large to have an outer entrance with a gate and for them to have servants.

Read Acts 12:13–15.
Who answered Peter's knock, and how did she respond to what she heard?

How did the praying believers respond to her news?

Due to their reaction, again, I do not think these believers were necessarily praying for Peter's deliverance, but for his peace and comfort while he awaited trial. I think they were praying for a speedy execution in which he would not have to endure much suffering. We see from their response that they had little to zero expectation for a miraculous intervention from prison. Ironically, Peter had already had a miraculous escape from jail back in Acts 5, so why did they not believe God could do it again?

Part of the reason may have been that his last escape had been from jail, which would have been less tightly secured than a Roman prison, and this time Peter was physically chained to Roman soldiers. Also, and more likely, their faith may have been badly shaken by the killing of James and fear as a whole gripped these believers, wondering which of them might be hauled off next to be executed. In their mind Peter was as good as dead. They were so certain of it that when Rhoda kept insisting Peter was at the door, their only logical explanation was that Peter had already been executed and it was his ghost.

Can you imagine Peter's thoughts as he stood outside the gate? Clamoring and arguing going on inside, while he fervently knocks outside, praying none of the neighbors wake up! He knocked loudly enough to overcome the heated discourse inside yet not too loudly. Makes me wonder. How many church meetings are spent in heated debate while Jesus stands at the door and knocks, waiting to be invited in? The miracle knocks at the door, but we are so busy proving our point to one another that nobody bothers to answer it.

Read Acts 12:16–19 and describe their reaction when they finally answered the door.

What did Peter command these believers to do?

We've already mentioned that James, John's brother, has been beheaded. This other James to whom Peter is now referring is Jesus' half-brother and the writer of the New Testament book of James. Historically, we know that he assumed leadership of the Jerusalem church. In this short exchange, Peter passes the baton to James as the new leader of the church. Peter is a wanted man and must go into hiding. Any believer's home in which he resided would have put them in danger of death. Where Peter fled remains unknown—possibly because Luke did not know where he went—or possibly to emphasize that none of the believers actually knew of Peter's whereabouts. Some scholars suggest he went to Rome and began to head up the church there.

How does Luke describe the reaction to Peter's escape?

What three actions did Herod take to try and find Peter?

Since Peter's guards were executed, we can ascertain that this was what Herod had intended to do to Peter. Under Roman law, if a guard or soldier lost their prisoner, they had to suffer the fate that the prisoner was intended to suffer. Although God delivered Peter, the Jerusalem church still needed to recover from his loss of leadership. We are not told what became of the rest of the believers whom Herod had arrested. It is likely Herod executed them along with the guards in his rage over being humiliated and outsmarted.

Despite this miraculous yet horrific chain of events, what are we told in Acts 12:24? Write this verse here:

Leaders are lost. Persecution arises. Fear attempts to overtake us. Yet in spite of it all, the Word of God continues to increase and spread! And so it will be to the end of the age. All of the fury of hell may come against the church of Jesus Christ, but His Word—and His church—will stand.

Turn to James 1 and read verses 1–6 penned by James, the same man that Peter passed the baton to in Acts 12:17.

What did James write about trials approximately five years after Peter's escape?

To what specific lack did James refer?

Once you ask, what must you do?

I wonder if James had this event in mind when he wrote the opening to his letter. The weight of the death of another man named James, Peter's imprisonment, escape, and subsequent departure must have felt daunting. Did he have enough wisdom to lead the church with them gone? Over and over he may have beseeched his risen brother for wisdom, still doubting his ability to effectively lead the church. A new era in church history was about to begin!

What is an area of your life for which you need wisdom?

In light of James's circumstances, how imminently did he need God to grant him wisdom?

As we can see, these young believers still lacked faith. They still needed much shepherding and instruction. As we close out this week, we will meet a young man of which this was certainly true. As we go out into the world to live unexplainable lives by the power of the Holy Spirit, we need to ask ourselves in what areas we are lacking. Then we need to trust that God is willing and able to provide us all that we need!

What is an area of your life for which you need greater faith right now?

Write a prayer here to ask your God for great faith in this area:

PORTRAIT OF A DISCIPLE —THE LIFE OF JOHN MARK

Please read aloud ACTS 12:19–25

The church in Jerusalem experienced great upheaval—martyrdom of a beloved brother, loss of leadership, and terror from every side. Yet the number of believers continued to grow! We also have a reminder that God sees everything from His throne in heaven and will only allow so much evil before responding.

Read Acts 12:19–23 and explain what happened to King Herod.

Luke again follows his bad news/good news pattern in his writing. The historian Josephus informs us that Herod's robes were shimmering silver, so when he stood up on a terrace to address the crowds and the sun struck the material, he glowed. I cannot miss the irony that the man who sought to destroy the church of the Son of God became struck down for claiming to be a god himself. Therein describes the essence of sin: replacing the rightful rule of Jesus in our lives with our desire to rule ourselves. And herein defines the essence of sin's results: death.

Whom did Saul and Barnabas take with them to Antioch (Acts 12:25)?

We are not told why they took John Mark with them back to Antioch. There could be many possibilities. His mother Mary, who was obviously a prominent figure in the Jerusalem church and offered her home for many church gatherings, may have persuaded Barnabas, who was John Mark's cousin, to do so in light of the outbreak of persecution among the Christians in Jerusalem. Another possibility could be that the death of James and the removal of Peter opened Paul's and Barnabas's eyes to the need to begin pouring into the next generation. The necessity to train up leaders became glaringly obvious when two apostles had been so swiftly removed. One thing is certain, they did not take him because he demonstrated incredible leadership skills. This young man needed effective discipling!

To have been selected to be a traveling companion of Paul and Barnabas would have been a tremendous honor. However, it also required hard work.

How is John Mark's role described in Acts 13:5?

Now look at verse 13. What did John Mark do in the middle of the missionary journey?

Turn to Acts 15:36–40. How does Luke later describe what happened on this missionary journey?

What did John Mark's desertion do to Paul and Barnabas's relationship?

What can we learn from John Mark's life so far? He came from a godly legacy—his mother was a devout and courageous believer, risking her very life in opening her home in Jerusalem for church gatherings. Thus far, John Mark does not exemplify his mother's courage nor her devotion. He had the opportunity to be mentored by two of the greatest leaders in church history. In the middle of this mentorship, he bailed out to return home to Jerusalem. His actions precipitated the dissolution of Paul and Barnabas's joint ministry and presumably their friendship as well.

Why does this guy get so much press on the pages of Scripture? So far he sounds like a train wreck! And if we are honest, our own fears can cause us to react in ways that cause us to miss out on God's grand adventures for our lives. They can also cause division among those whom we love, because we behave in selfish ways when we are governed by fear.

Describe a time in your life when you made a decision out of fear and you later regretted it:

John Mark's life is going to teach us that our past mistakes do not define our future. They can impact our future: either positively or negatively, depending on what we choose to learn from them. We have only scratched the surface of John Mark's life. He has much to learn and a long way to go, but God is not finished with him yet. And He's not finished with you and me. Maybe you and I need to uncover what fear keeps us from truly living unexplainable lives.

What are some fears that you currently battle today?

Who ends up being John Mark's primary mentor in Acts 15:39?

Why do you suppose Barnabas would be a more effective mentor for a young man who battles with fear than Paul?

I believe John Mark loved Jesus. I believe he wanted to follow Him with everything in him, but his fear held him back. A fearless follower like Paul surely inspired John Mark, but also made him feel defeated. His mind filled with thoughts: "Why can't I be brave like that? Why can't I speak with conviction, fearless of anyone's response?" John Mark needed a Barnabas, somebody to remind him, "You have the Holy Spirit, John Mark, you will get there! Just keep following Jesus!" He needed an encourager.

God knows exactly who or what we need as well. However, we have to be intentional about finding them. If we do not regularly engage with the body of believers in Bible study, small groups, or service projects, it becomes very difficult for us to connect with these mentors God has for us. If we are not regularly allowing the Holy Spirit to guide and teach us through God's Word, it becomes difficult to discern the truth about what others say about us.

As we will see tomorrow, Paul was a powerhouse of a man of God, but he was wrong about John Mark. It took Barnabas to see John Mark's potential. If someone in your past has written you off or counted you out, it does not mean you have to stay there. Just because they have given up on you doesn't mean that God has.

The very man who originally gave up on John Mark later wrote the words of Philippians 1:6. Write them below:

Paul composed this letter about fifteen to twenty years after his dispute with Barnabas over John Mark. It sounds like he had a change of heart. And as we will discover tomorrow, so does John Mark, because we will see a new man—a faithful and fearless follower of Jesus living an unexplainable life!

WEEK 10 DAY 5
PORTRAIT OF A DISCIPLE CONTINUED—JOHN MARK AND YOU!

Please read aloud VARIOUS PASSAGES

Paul departed with Silas while Barnabas headed out with John Mark. A split in relationship resulted from John Mark's fearful flee three years prior, but a multiplication of missionaries also occurs. Again we see Luke emphasize how difficulty can bring about positive results in the overall spread of Jesus' church.

Have you ever seen God bring good from a disagreement among believers? If so, describe the situation:

If devout and godly men like Paul and Barnabas can fall into disagreement with each other, we ought to be realistic about the chances of division occurring within our churches. These men were 100 percent sold out for Jesus in every aspect of their lives, but they were not perfect or above making mistakes. We must constantly pray for unity among believers. It is another reminder to pray fervently for our church leadership!

What admonitions did Paul give the church in Ephesians 4:2–3 and in Colossians 3:12–14?

Luke does not tell us how John Mark and Paul became reunited. Each man needed to ask for forgiveness from the other—John Mark for deserting Paul in the middle of the journey and Paul for writing John Mark off. Surely Paul's life lesson in seeing the work of God in John Mark's life influenced him. We see the result of that influence many years later in his epistles.

What else did Paul command the Colossian believers to do in regard to John Mark? See Colossians 4:10.

How else does Paul describe John Mark in Philemon 24?

It is obvious that Barnabas's investment in John Mark's life paid off. He is still functioning as a missionary twenty years later, traveling around to the churches, no doubt to encourage them as he had learned from his faithful mentor. It would be one thing for Paul and John Mark to reconcile, but what I will show you next is even more unexplainable.

What does Paul ask in 2 Timothy 4:11?

Now this just thrills me! Here is Paul nearing the end of his life. He knows he will soon die. And for whom does he ask? John Mark. Think about the people you'll want by your side as you near death. Presumably those you love most in the world, those to whom you wish to impart the most sacred of wisdom and instruction. A small, intimate few. Your legacy. Paul had ministered to countless thousands during his lifetime, but John Mark was counted among his legacy.

Paul called him useful. No doubt he wanted to disclose certain instructions to John Mark to carry on the work of the Lord after his departure. Paul recognized John Mark's knowledge and love for the churches. He knew he could be entrusted to continue to care for them. For the past twenty years John Mark had continued to travel from church to church, developing strong bonds with the believers. What a beautiful picture of restoration and redemption. I cannot wait to hear the full story in heaven one day!

What we also see here is the symbiosis in their relationship. While early in John Mark's life he needed only to learn from Paul, it is at this juncture that Paul needs John Mark to serve him. While Paul sat in prison thinking back over his life and all of his exploits and life lessons, it was at this time that he had the most wisdom to share. John Mark could have said, "No, I would rather continue traveling around to the churches than sit in a prison cell with Paul," but he would have missed out on some of Paul's most profound teachings. These teachings are embodied in Paul's epistles to the churches. We don't know, but it's possible John Mark may sometimes have even functioned as a scribe for Paul.

How does Peter describe John Mark in 1 Peter 5:13?

Despite his previous actions, John Mark developed into one of the great leaders of the early church. Dearly loved by Paul and Peter, he also became entrusted with the sacred task of recording what is traditionally believed to be the earliest gospel. After a rough start marked by fear and mistakes, John Mark grew into a faithful and fearless follower of our Lord! So what about you and me?

Who would consider you to be a part of their legacy? Who will want you by their side when it's all said and done?

Who would call you their "true son/daughter" in the faith as Peter referred to John Mark?

Who is part of your legacy and what are doing to pour into them?

Who has encouraged you to become a faithful and fearless follower of the Lord? How can you honor them?

If you feel as though you need more encouragement, how can you intentionally seek out mentors? (A great resource on this topic is *Face to Face: Discover How Mentoring Can Change Your Life* by Jayme Hull.)

Who are you encouraging?

You and I were given the Holy Spirit when we received Jesus as our Savior. We may still need a little time and encouragement to become as faithful and fearless as John Mark, but if God is for us, who can be against us? God made Peter bold in fifty days, but it took ten years to break through the constraints of his upbringing. Paul needed about ten years to temper his zeal and develop a pastoral heart. John Mark also took over a decade, possibly even two, to become the man God created him to be. Our faith walk is a journey—we already know our destination, so today it's about moving in the right direction!

We also have the Word of God and our fellow Christians, to encourage, develop, strengthen, and shape us into the disciples we were intended to be. So what are you waiting for? You have everything you need to take the first step on your journey toward an unexplainable life! Let's get going! We don't want our lives to be marked by a substitute power or temporary satisfaction, do we? Consider what A. W. Tozer says:

> We may as well face it: the whole level of spirituality among us is low.
> We have measured ourselves by ourselves until the incentive to seek
> higher plateaus in the things of the Spirit is all but gone . . . we have imitated
> the world, sought popular favor, manufactured delights to substitute
> for the joy of the Lord and produced a cheap and synthetic power to
> substitute for the power of the Holy Ghost.[22]

Friend, you and I have discovered the power of the Holy Spirit during the last fifty days together. We understand our need to invite Him into our lives and churches to do the unexplainable. He is the One who transforms us! Before you close your book for our final day together, let's be brave enough together to ask the Lord some tough questions.

Lord, what is holding me back from being the faithful and fearless follower I know in my heart I want to be?

Who or what have I believed about myself that has caused me to give up pursuing You fully with my life?

Who could I ask to invest in me or in whom could I invest to build into the spiritual legacy of the church?

Now write down one specific action step you will take after completing this study:

Write out your prayer of commitment to follow the Lord and allow the Holy Spirit to lead you in living an unexplainable life:

Be blessed this day, dear one! I hope to journey with you again soon. It was my joy and privilege to travel alongside you. Praying for unexplainable lives for all of us!

SOME PARTING THOUGHTS

The work of the Holy Spirit in and through the church continues today. The incredible story of Jesus' church had only just begun in Acts 1–12. You and I are the church. We are the people through whom He desires to work and He has something in mind for each of us! Oh, how gloriously patient He is with us! He sees not just who we are, but who we shall become as we allow Him to have His way with us. Though we collectively close this fifty-day study today, it is truly just the beginning for all of us. The work He began within our heart and mind upon salvation, He will carry to completion and it will surely be unexplainable!

Persecution, beginning with Stephen's martyrdom, played a pivotal role in the expansion of the church. In our time we see persecution on the rise. It is important to remember these early believers and remind ourselves that God will continue to send His church forth. Nothing will come against it either inside or out that will be able to stop the name of Jesus being spread. We are not to fear—God has already won! While God miraculously delivered Peter for future ministry, He delivered John's brother James through death. Either way, we are delivered into the arms of our Savior.

Think of it—you and I are the result of these fearless early believers carrying the gospel forth. Passed down through generations too many to count, the gospel message came to us. And now the message is ours—in peace, in prosperity, in persecution, and in doubt. Will you and I be faithful to pass it along to the generations after us?

We began our journey with Peter standing in the shadows denying Jesus, to his standing in the temple courts boldly preaching. Several years later, the Holy Spirit transforms Peter's life again by removing his cultural and religious preconceptions allowing him to extend the gospel to the Gentiles. Pentecost was only the beginning for Peter. Our fifty days together was only the beginning for you and me.

You, dear one, have an amazing adventure ahead. It's our turn. Now *we* must go.

We are the church. It's our time. Let's invite God to do something unexplainable!

I'd love to hear what our great God is doing in and through you by the power of His marvelous Holy Spirit. There is no greater joy than sharing our God stories, being once again filled with wonder at His Person and His power! Please share yours with me at ericawiggenhorn.com or on social media using #unexplainable.

Fill us, Holy Spirit, and open our minds to understand Your Word!

—Erica

NOTES

1. A. W. Tozer, *Who Put Jesus on the Cross?* (Camp Hill, PA: Wingspread, 2009), Kindle edition.

2. Francis Chan, *Forgotten God: Reversing Our Tragic Neglect of the Holy Spirit* (Colorado Springs: David C Cook, 2009), 142.

3. N. T. Wright, *Acts for Everyone Part 1* (Louisville: Westminster John Knox Press, 2008), 14.

4. H. A. Ironside, *Acts* (Grand Rapids: Kregal, 2007), 18.

5. The Complete Jewish Bible by David H. Stern. Copyright © 1998. All rights reserved. Used by permission of Messianic Jewish Publishers, 6120 Day Long Lane, Clarksville, MD 21029. www.messianicjewish.net.

6. Chan, *Forgotten God: Reversing Our Tragic Neglect of the Holy Spirit*, 120.

7. Wright, *Acts for Everyone Part 1*, 39.

8. http://www.evanwiggs.com/revival/history/hebpray.html.

9. Ironside, *Acts*, 59.

10. Matthew Henry, *Matthew Henry's Commentary* (Grand Rapids: Zondervan, 1961), 1650.

11. Craig S. Keener, *The IVP Bible Background Commentary New Testament* (Downers Grove: Inter-Varsity Press), 280.

12. Henry, *Matthew Henry's Commentary*, 1649.

13. Keener, *The IVP Bible Background Commentary New Testament*, 335.

14. Brice C. Jones, "The Meaning of the Phrase 'And the Witnesses Laid Down Their Cloaks' in Acts 7:58," *The Expository Times* 123 (2011): 113–118, accessed November 26, 2015, doi:10.1177/0014524611421729.

15. Ibid.

16. Spiros Zodhiates, trans. *The Hebrew-Greek Key Study Bible* (Grand Rapids: Baker Book House, 1984), 53.

17. The Amplified® Bible, Copyright © 1954, 1958, 1962, 1964, 1965, 1987 by The Lockman Foundation. Used by permission. (www.Lockman.org).

18. John MacArthur, *Acts 1–12*, The MacArthur New Testament Commentary Series (Chicago: Moody, 1994), 251.

19. Wright, *Acts for Everyone Part 1*, 138–39.

20. Zodhiates, *The Hebrew-Greek Key Study Bible*, 1706.

21. Ibid., 1687.

22. A. W. Tozer, *Of God and Men* (Chicago: Moody, 2015), 15.

ACKNOWLEDGMENTS

The Head of the church, our precious Lord and Savior Jesus Christ, who offers us unexplainable grace. I humbly lay this work at Your feet.

My family, for taking this unexplainable journey with me! I wouldn't want to travel with anyone else! You keep me on the right road and are my true joy.

My friends, whose prayers, encouragement, and endless offers of help made this study possible.

Tami Engram, my prayer warrior, who walked alongside me and reminded me daily to bring this project to the altar.

Charis Women of Desert Springs, who have taught me a million times more than I have ever shared with them.

Judy Dunagan, a woman who exemplifies an unexplainable life. Thank you for listening to the whisper of the Spirit. I pray He is well pleased with this work. Pam Pugh, whose editing transformed this work—thank you for your diligence. The entire team at Moody Publishers who exhibit the Spirit of Christ in all they say and do.

To every reader who made a commitment to exalt our Lord in the diligent study of His Word—I am humbled and honored to journey alongside you. Thank you for granting me the privilege.

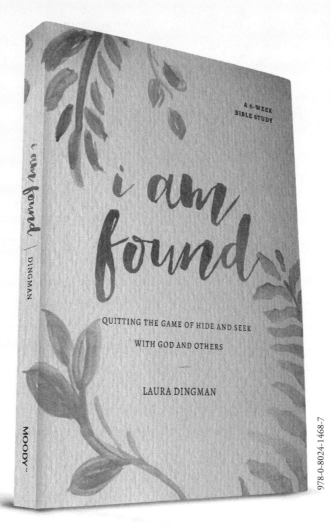

Discipleship Resources

978-0-8024-1382-6   978-0-8024-1343-7   978-0-8024-1340-6

Moody Publishers is committed to providing powerful, biblical, and life-changing discipleship resources for women. Our prayer is that these resources will cause a ripple effect of making disciples who make disciples who make disciples.

Also available as ebooks

MOODY
Publishers™

From the Word to Life

From the Word *to Life*

Moody Radio produces and delivers compelling programs filled with biblical insights and creative expressions of faith that help you take the next step in your relationship with Christ.

You can hear Moody Radio on 36 stations and more than 1,500 radio outlets across the U.S. and Canada. Or listen on your smartphone with the Moody Radio app!

www.moodyradio.org